Perspectives From The Pitch

A Basic Guide to Understanding Soccer
Commands and Appreciating How They
Apply to Life
Lou Roth

In memory of my parents, George and Edda, who fostered in me a curiosity about the world

Dedicated to Tami, who has supported me throughout this journey, and to Brendan, Devin, Morgan, and Connor, my children, who are an endless source of joy and inspiration

Contents

PREFACE: PRE-GAME WARM-UPS   1

SECTION ONE: ATTACKING   5

1. DRIBBLE   6
    Appreciating that freedom yields growth

2. FIRST TOUCH   11
    Preparing to start in the right direction

3. TURN   16
    The importance of awareness

4. GET IN THE LIGHT   20
    The need for curiosity, focus, and engagement

5. PLAY TO FEET   24
    Getting the details right

6. PLAY TO SPACE   27
    Taking advantage of opportunities

7. HEELS ON THE TOUCHLINE   31
    Seeing things from a different perspective

8. KNOW WHAT TO DO WITH THE BALL BEFORE   36
    YOU GET IT
    Planning ahead to breed confidence

9. DON'T RUN AWAY   41
    The importance of relationships

10. KEEP IT   47
    Controlling how we respond to challenges

11. KEEP IT MOVING   51
    Purpose guides decisions

12. TIME   56
    Prioritize how to spend time

13. CARRY (TAKE YOUR SPACE)   61
    Stepping outside your comfort zone

14. RELAX   64
    Remaining calm in chaotic moments

15. GO HOME   70
    Keeping options open

WATER BREAK: POSSESSION FOR DEVELOP-   74
MENT

SECTION TWO: DEFENDING   81

16. CONTAIN (DON'T DIVE IN)   82
    Assessing a problem in order to solve it

17. DON'T FOUL   86
    Remember the big picture

18. LOCK THEM IN   90
    Taking calculated risks

19. WIN SOMETHING   94
    Defining who we become through consistency

20. BOUNCING BALL   97
    Taking notice of things

21. WHEN ONE GOES, WE ALL GO   101
    Taking initiative

22. MARK UP   106
    Embracing responsibility

23. HOLD THE 18   110
    Enough is enough

24. AWAY - BE SAFE - CLEAR IT   113
    The wisdom of prudential decisions

WATER BREAK: TOTAL FOOTBALL   116

SECTION THREE: TRANSITION   121

25. FIRST MAN   122
    The importance of responding to a mistake

26. GET BEHIND THE BALL   126
    The importance of quick reactions

27. 50-50   130
    Committing to challenges

28. SECOND BALL   134
    Seeing the bigger picture and understanding your role

29. DON'T BALL WATCH   138
    Remembering priorities

30. MAKE THE SIMPLE PASS   144
    Restoring order

31. NEXT FIVE   149

    Staying even-keeled

WATER BREAK: SPREAD OUT   152

CONCLUSION: POST-GAME TALK   155

INJURY TIME   159

Acknowledgements   161

PREFACE: PRE-GAME WARM-UPS

———————— ⚽ ————————

Soccer is the world's game. Here in America, over 6,000,000 kids play organized soccer. Major League Soccer currently has 30 teams, most with their own dedicated stadiums and average over 20,000 fans per game - rivaling the NHL in many markets. European football (particularly the English Premier League) has surged in popularity among fans in the United States. You're just as likely to see a Liverpool or Arsenal jersey as an NFL jersey in any American city.

At some point, nearly all kids get some experience playing soccer. For some, it may be just a few weeks in their physical education classes. Others may play for just a season in their formative years, while a few play through their childhood and continue on into adulthood.

It's a game that requires only a ball and space to play, so that some variation of the game is open to anyone; to simply play the game there is no socioeconomic or racial barrier. Different levels of the game make the sport available for those with different abilities. As a result, soccer offers the same lessons for elite players as it does for those with limited ability to play. *The game is the same.*

Despite the boon in popularity, there is still a lack of understanding regarding the sport, as it relates to styles of play, basic tactics, youth development, and even why kids play the game. **This book is designed not only to give general insight into the intricacies of the game, but also to highlight some important life lessons that can be learned from playing. I've**

written it in the hopes that parents, coaches, and players will recognize that the sport offers lessons that transcend the time actually spent on the field. It's important to realize that the vast majority of youth players will <u>not</u> become professionals or even collegiate athletes. The point, however, is that no matter what sporting level a child ultimately reaches, there are so many parallels between the game of soccer and the game of life. Coaches and parents have a responsibility to develop the <u>whole</u> person – not just the athlete. The game offers so much, and like anything else in life, we take out of it what we put into it.

The game of soccer is continuous and moves too quickly for the coach (or parents) to dictate the movements of each player for the duration of the game. Young players need to learn the answers to the game's problems, but like anything else, the learning doesn't become permanent until they figure it out on their own. Athletes need to be encouraged to work out how to solve problems in different ways. Just as players can't be controlled by a coach with a joystick, there comes a time when the decisions kids make will be their own. Soccer provides that opportunity for kids to learn the responsibility that comes from making their own decisions.

So, what is the role of the coach? It is up to coaches to help inspire their young charges and to cultivate each player's passion for their sport. We all want to raise hard-working, responsible kids who learn to think on their own.

I grew up as one of "Pele's kids" who fell in love with the game playing youth soccer in the 1970s and 80s. At that time, my coaches were volunteers with just a rudimentary knowledge of the game. Still, I loved it, eventually becoming an avid fan. As I got older, I learned more and more about the game, and I wanted to share that knowledge with others. As a youth soccer coach and a father of kids who played, I've seen countless opportunities to relate the game to life. I've spent many hours driving in the car to and from tournaments with my kids, which I found to be a great time for longer, deeper conversations. While I never liked to re-hash the game with them, as we talked about other parts of their lives, I found that game situations could be pretty relatable allegories. I started thinking more about that and began to see how the game could be a conduit for imparting positive messages.

In today's world, youth sports often provide one of the few outlets where kids can develop somewhat independently. Given the nature of the sport, soccer offers perhaps the best opportunity to do so. With no timeouts and limited substitutions, it really is a player's game. The capacity to make one's own decisions and accept the consequences is a critical piece of personal development, and the best coaches recognize this.

COACHING PROMPTS

In most team sports, coaches use specific instructions (e.g., a diagrammed play in American football or basketball that outlines the job of every player). In soccer, however, prompts are better than detailed instructions. Specific instructions just tell a kid what to do, so there is no need for them to think for themselves. Prompts or challenges, on the other hand, help to paint a picture for a player and to orient them in their environment. They enable a player to sense the challenges as well as the possibilities he is facing at that moment. The important part, though, is that the prompts give a kid enough information to solve the problem in his own way.

That's the purpose of this book: to highlight a handful of such prompts and explain how they give a player the opportunity to creatively solve a challenge, and how to extend that knowledge to situations they may face off the soccer field. This form of self-instruction (with guidance from a coach) is the best way to learn, develop, and retain the lessons provided by the game.

As children grow up, they often recognize coaches they had as playing particularly important roles in their development not only as players, but as people. Coaches in all sports acknowledge that they not only impact athletic performance, but they have an opportunity to guide kids and teach life lessons. I've often heard that phrase, "life lessons through sport," but how can it be done so that those lessons really sink in for a young player?

The instructions that coaches call out during the game are usually brief and direct, but there is a deeper meaning behind those simple instructions. As a player develops and learns different ways to solve problems, he can understand that the cues offered by a coach can be applied to more than just the soccer field. This book takes a few of the common coaching prompts used in soccer and provides examples of what they could mean in someone's life outside the game.

In addition, you'll notice I've inserted a few "water breaks" at the end of each section to make a few observations about youth soccer development in general.

SECTION ONE: ATTACKING

"I don't believe skill was, or ever will be, the result of coaches. It is a result of a love affair between the child and the ball."
– Manfred Schellscheidt, U.S. Soccer Hall of Famer

Chapter 1

DRIBBLE

Appreciating that freedom yields growth

"My first question is always 'can this player dribble?' I only want players who have that skill. I want fullbacks, centerbacks, forwards who can dribble. You can learn control and passing easily, so dribbling is key." – Pep Guardiola, Coach at Manchester City

It's no surprise that the first things young players learn are the technical components of the game. Fortunately, all players enjoy playing with the ball. Particularly at younger ages, kids *want* to dribble the ball. In their initial years, practices should be "one player, one ball," where the kids play a variety of games (not drills) and learn how to manipulate the ball. Ideally, at these younger ages the kids play on a small field with very few players, (3v3 or 4v4). As they grow, the field gets bigger and the number of players increases, thus offering more opportunities and challenges – as we'll see later.

Regardless of age, though, all athletes naturally tend to remain focused on their own game, but this is even more acute at the youngest ages. The worldview of small children is much different than an adult's. It's narrowly self-focused, and when they play a game (even on a team), they want to play with the ball. It's a completely natural thing. In a team setting, when they get "their turn" with the ball, of course they want to play with it.

GAME SCENARIO

This is why they often get confused when a well-meaning grown-up yells "BOOT IT!" because – Heaven forbid – the child is dribbling the ball near his own goal and might give it away. Notwithstanding the obvious point that a child giving a goal away in a U7 game really doesn't matter in the great scheme of things, the young player needs to express himself and begin learning how to manipulate the ball so he can improve over time.

Parents screaming on the sidelines, "You're going the wrong way!" or "No! Not backwards!" are missing the point. By "booting" the ball or clearing it away, he is likely giving the ball to the other team anyway. Worse, he is giving up the responsibility of finding a solution to the problem he's facing. In a sense, he is giving up the accountability of playing; he's passing the buck to someone else and playing in a cowardly manner. Young players who try (and try again) to improve on the ball and gain confidence to maneuver out of sticky situations are learning bravery and developing a willingness to take on harder challenges. This is something that every child needs. We want to foster bravery in our kids. We want them to grow in confidence and express themselves. Kids need to know that it's OK if they make mistakes, because that's when they really learn. If they're too afraid to make mistakes on a soccer field, they probably won't try new things in other areas of their life.

As kids get older and play with more players on bigger fields, they will learn to see tactical problems and find solutions; they will improve in their decision-making skills and understand when and where to try a special dribbling move. But they'll never be able to get to that point if at a young age all they hear is "DON'T DRIBBLE!" Let the kid be brave and don't stifle his creativity. Remember, the soccer ball is a wonderful toy. Let them play with it as they want to!

Will there be setbacks — maybe giving up a goal or losing a game? Sure — but if a kid has it beaten out of him to not take chances when playing sports, he won't take many in life.

As adults, we know that there are times when you have to go it alone. Players can't be afraid to try something when presented with the opportunity; they must be encouraged to be brave on the field, because cultivating an attacking mindset is really important.

People get excited watching a good dribbler run through a defense, or when a player pulls out a few moves to get himself out of trouble and create some space for his teammates. Over the last 10 to 15 years, people all over the world have fawned over the great teams of Barcelona and their "tiki-taka" style of short, simple passes. Yet even Barcelona at its peak with their fluid passing style still needed dribblers like Lionel Messi and Andres Iniesta to break down defenses. If you don't think so, see Pep Guardiola's quote above.

Obviously, not everyone can dribble like Messi. But dribbling remains the foundation of all other skills; mastery of the ball is paramount for any player as it is the clear foundation for everything in the game. Comfort on the ball gives players more time to think about what they're going to do next.

I'd like to add a note here about coaching prompts. As a general rule, coaches should not give instructions to players while they have the ball at their feet. Not only does it confuse the player (his perspective gives him his own idea of what he should do), but it diminishes the child's ability to think for himself. He can't learn to think for himself if he is told what to do all the time. This can be a hard realization for the adults watching, but giving kids the freedom to play and make their own decisions should start at an early age.

LIFE OBSERVATION

This applies off the field as well. Obviously, we don't let kids put themselves in danger – but they need some degree of freedom in order to grow. Coaxing out thought processes and helping kids develop the ability and willingness to make the right decisions is an essential part of growing up. Think about all the decisions we as adults have to make every day, from the trivial (what shoes to wear) to the significant (should I accept that job offer?).

How we make decisions stems from thought processes and mental patterns we have developed from childhood. Those times we explored our neighborhood or chose what friends to play with presented opportunities to grow as people and to learn how to make smart decisions. Freedom and independence (both in time and play) is incredibly valuable to youth development and personal growth.

The trouble, however, is that as today's parents zealously seek to secure a child's prosperous future, something has gone missing. While there have always been parents who push their kids too much (and/or try to live vicariously through them), it is important to remember that it is the child's life and not the adult's. Without the opportunities for independent, personal growth, a child's development can stagnate.

More and more today, for a multitude of reasons – from safety concerns to ambitious parents, kids in contemporary society don't have the opportunities to play and learn on their own (from both their successes and failures) as kids of past generations did. Yes, they are extremely busy – *organized* team practices, *organized* music lessons, *organized* play dates, etc. This hyper-militarized level of organization has become endemic. The research related to this over-structured lifestyle of our youth has been chronicled elsewhere – and the results are not good.[1]

As kids grow up in environments where adults tell them what to do at practically all times of the day, the lack of free time can have seriously negative consequences. Among a number of problems, overly structured environments prevent the development of self-introspection, hamper the ability to think creatively, limit opportunities to make decisions – and more importantly, accept the consequences of those decisions (good or bad) — and contribute to the decline of socialization skills.

On a soccer field, with a ball at his feet, a child has freedom and experiences the joy of it. The fresh air, the smell of the grass, watching the ground rush by under your feet as you maneuver through players with echoes of shouts ringing in your ears...there's nothing like dribbling. For a child's growth as a player and a person, let them experience that freedom to make their own decisions and learn from them. It's important for his own personal development, and honestly, it's just a lot of fun.

"Freedom is nothing but a chance to be better." – Albert Camus

---

1. Siobhan O'Connor, "The Secret Power of Play," *Time*, September 6, 2017, https://time.com/4928925/secret-power-play/

Chapter 2

FIRST TOUCH

———— ⚽ ————

Preparing to start in the right direction

"Everything I know about morality and the obligations of men I owe to football...I learned...that a ball never comes from the direction you were expecting it." – Albert Camus

As kids mature and begin playing with more players on bigger fields, new problems – and opportunities – await them. The importance of playing with your teammates becomes more evident, and the ability to give and take passes successfully becomes paramount.

While players in every sport are evaluated by basic techniques (e.g., hitting a baseball or throwing a football), the first impression of a soccer player is her first touch, that is, her ability to control a ball regardless of how it's played to her (especially when under pressure). Since a good first touch is necessary to do anything in the game, it is a basic technique that players must master.

GAME SCENARIO

A player's ability to recognize and understand what's around her, coupled with a good first touch, helps the player make the best decision possible for the team.

With a bad first touch, however, the player is at best looking for a safe pass...and at worst is likely to turn the ball over. In general, the overall ability of a team's first touch is typically indicative of a team's technical ability. Given this fact, you would think that a player's first touch and all that goes with it would be a primary focus of a youth coach.

After all, a player's first touch provides vital information to her teammates, coaches, and the opposition. From a development perspective, a good, technical first touch is required before *any* tactical objective can be achieved. If a coach wants her young charges to play out of the back, the defenders need a good first touch. If a player takes too many touches to control the ball, the sequence will likely fail. If midfielders are directed to switch the field (swing the ball from one side of the field to the other), a good first touch is necessary. I could go on and on.

The technical aspect of receiving is developed through repetition at practice, under situations involving increasing pressure. A crucial ingredient that must not be overlooked, however, is the education about the thought process behind a first touch. A player has to consider what technique is necessary so that her first touch will give her the time and space she needs to make the next play. Understanding the situation and knowing what the next play should be is all part of training. With a positive first touch, a player and her teammates can dictate the tempo of a game. A good first touch can improve the speed of play; it is also a prerequisite for the decision to slow down the game in the appropriate situation.

One thing that coaches try to instill in young players is **the necessity of knowing what you're going to do with the ball before you get it**. The need for constant awareness is absolutely crucial to soccer players, and a coach can assess this based on the direction of a player's first touch.

The first touch is illustrative of how a player sees the game. Her spatial awareness, her confidence, her technical ability, her bravery, and her decision-making ability are all there in this one touch. That's why small-sided games are so important. When coaches let kids play these games, kids have the opportunity to experiment and refine their technique, develop their awareness, and hone their decision-making skills. Coaches benefit as it becomes easier to assess and correct these same elements.

A player's first touch is the key that opens the door and allows the coach to get a glimpse into what the player's decision-making is based upon.

The player's first touch can be seen as a statement of intent. It's directional and has purpose. When I was a kid, coaches would teach us to "trap" a ball (to basically stop it dead). The problem with this is that it isolates the player from the broader context of the game. It doesn't take the player's situation into account. It's static rather than dynamic.

It's somewhat robotic – a player would "trap," or control the ball, and then decide what to do. Contrast this with a first touch, where the ball doesn't stop moving as the player takes the ball where she wants to go. Thankfully, coaching in the US has evolved.

The dynamic directional movement in a good first touch forces other players to react. The first touch may be to wheel away from danger, or slow the game down, or it may indicate an aggressive attack on goal. Regardless, it reveals a player's intentions.

As mentioned previously, a good first touch should be a priority for all youth coaches. The confidence that comes from the trained ability to control and manipulate the ball the way a player wants to is priceless.

LIFE OBSERVATION

As Camus noted in the quote that opened this chapter, the ball may come to you in a way you don't expect. The same is true in life. If you can deal with a situation with a good first touch, you have the potential to turn something bad into something positive. If a defender sees an opponent preparing to receive a difficult ball, she may think that it will take time for that opponent to get the ball under control. But if the receiving player can do something unexpected (like execute a challenging turn to create space or play a difficult one-time pass to spring a sudden breakaway), then a potentially negative situation has been turned on its head.

We want to develop confidence in kids, to grow and believe in themselves. Because we know that life is full of unexpected trials, we also seek to foster a strong mindset, a positive attitude that will help them to become willing to take on such challenges.

One thing that the age of social media has really made manifest is that there are plenty of people in the world who love to complain about things, rather than accept challenges that come and try to solve them. This world certainly needs more people who are willing to tackle problems. These individuals become leaders, as they have the foresight to see opportunities that exist behind the problems.

The kid who, while contending with a difficult bouncing ball yet tries a tricky one-time pass, is making a bold statement about her own self-belief. She believes she can make that pass even though she's in a tough spot, and she thinks she can help the team gain an advantage.

Your decisions and actions in life serve as a declaration of your intentions. In a soccer game, the first touch reveals a player's thought process. Awareness and decisiveness are key. In life, having a plan and knowing what you want to do in given situations enables you to act appropriately. Thinking ahead and planning for contingencies can give you an advantage in life. What do I do if I don't get into the college I want? What if I were laid off or forced to take a pay cut? Awareness, preparation, and intent allows you to be decisive when the moment arises.

Again, this attitude is something we want to encourage in young players, because how they play in a game will transfer to how they approach life. If they believe they can overcome a challenge on a soccer field, chances are that they can conquer problems off the field as well.

"We cannot direct the wind, but we can adjust the sails." – Dolly Parton

Chapter 3

TURN

———— ⚽ ————

The importance of awareness

"Every good, successful player, especially an attacking player, has a well-developed sense of space and time." – Thomas Muller, midfielder for Bayern Munich and Germany

You can picture the scene: A coach yells, "TURN!" as a young player, standing in midfield, has just received the ball from a defender and is facing his own goal. Without having checked his shoulder, he isn't sure about his options. While he was always fairly comfortable on the ball, his coach knew that he often opted to play it safe and tended to pass the ball backwards or sideways – even if he had time and space to carry the ball forward. The coach wanted him to take the responsibility to change direction and dribble the ball into the space that was available, rather than merely play one- or two-touch passes.

Good coaches spend a fair amount of time on turning techniques in practice and encourage their players to try those moves in games. A key component to this is confidence, but what happens before the turn is just as important. Simply looking around, checking over the shoulders, and being aware of what is near a player on the field is the first (and necessary) part of the decision.

GAME SCENARIO

One effective tool is receiving the ball on the "half-turn." This is simply a positional stance whereby the receiving player faces the ball in a way that makes it easy to connect with both the attackers and the defenders. Most young players in the middle of the field are often forced to make a full 180-degree turn because they receive the ball fully facing their own goal.

Receiving the ball on the half-turn affords a player the opportunity to see much more of the field. If you are square to the passer, often your only real option is to return the ball where it came from because your field of vision is limited. Receiving on the half-turn allows you to take your first touch forward, rather than backwards.

Good players develop the ability to constantly scan the space around them in order to see where their positioning is relative to teammates and opponents. This awareness of space can make all the difference for a player.

The concept of space is something that coaches think a lot about as they try to get kids to understand the game. The reason is that space is one of the two basic elements of the sport. Time is the other.

As parents, we always want our kids to be more aware of their surroundings, to see what's around them and understand the environment that they are in. If, as Woody Allen said, 90% of life is showing up, it is critical for our kids to be able to acknowledge and interpret what is happening around them so they may be able to understand potential implications of their decisions and so make good choices.

This is what a coach tries to instill in his soccer players – *awareness.* A player must know where he is on the field in relation to the ball, as well as where his teammates and opponents are, in order to figure out how best to help his team. If his team has the ball, can he find a "seam" on the field between opposing players where he could receive a pass in a good position? He's always asking himself, "Where is the space?"

This is where his own vision and initiative come into play. He certainly can't be limited by position; the principles of the game should take clear precedence over simple positional restrictions forced on him by a coach. The ball is always moving; young players need to rapidly calculate where in the playing area they need to be in order to impact the game. The picture is always changing, and so are the decisions that players need to be making.

Soccer, like life, can be very chaotic, and as a result the game is decided in part by who can make order out of it and who can exploit the space on the field to their advantage. The world's best players make short, smart runs to find pockets of space between defenders. This space that a player receives the ball in gives him the precious commodity of time, which allows him to make the next play.

Regardless of any specific position, coaches need to ensure that all players understand the concept of space (and awareness of it), in order that their players can better affect the outcome of a game.

LIFE OBSERVATION

The need to be aware of your environment is even more important off the field. If you are alert and aware of what's happening around you, then you are open to both opportunities and challenges. You can position yourself to be prepared for whatever happens. On the soccer field, self-awareness makes you think; do you have the skill required to execute the proper action (i.e., return a pass or turn)? Have you as a player trained for this situation? Can you execute the best skill that will help you and your teammates achieve an objective?

Whether in school, work, or social situations – are you thinking about what could happen and are you prepared to act in a certain way?

As soccer is a team sport, game situations feature multiple variables (living, breathing variables!). The environment is constantly changing. What wasn't there five seconds ago may be there now – and this changes the dynamic significantly. When you are about to receive a ball, who can help you? Where are your teammates? Who is trying to stop you? Who wants you to make the wrong decision? What is your solution to the problems they pose?

Awareness and preparation are the keys.

"With awareness come responsibility and choice." – Amanda Lindhout, Canadian humanitarian and journalist

Chapter 4

GET IN THE LIGHT

———— ⚽ ————

The need for curiosity, focus, and engagement

"In football, the worst blindness is only seeing the ball." – Nelson Falcao Rodrigues, Brazilian sportswriter

When coaches try to help young players to understand how to use space effectively, one of the simplest concepts they try to impose is the idea of "light" versus "dark."

GAME SCENARIO

Players should always be seeking to create numerical advantages all over the field. Having numbers in your favor is obviously beneficial when trying to keep the ball. The most basic of these is 2v1. If one player has the ball, her nearby teammate can help her by "showing" for a pass. This extra player creates a dilemma for the defender, who now has to watch for an extra player.

This second player only helps, however, if she is "open," that is, if there is a clear path between the passer and the receiver. If the defender positions herself between the attackers – thereby blocking the path between them – then the second player is taken out of the play and the 2v1 is now a 1v1.

Standing behind the defender, the second attacker has put herself, "in the dark," or "in the shadow." This is when a coach may remind the second attacker to "get in the light" – to position herself so that there is a clear path for the ball carrier to pass the ball to her.

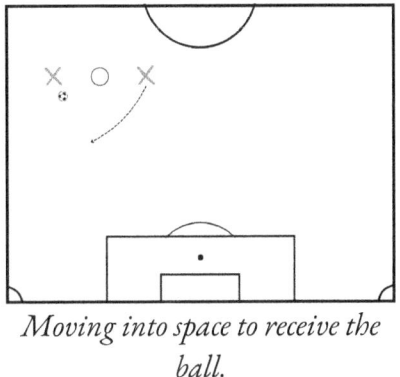

Moving into space to receive the
ball.

Getting in the light and out of the shadow is a great reminder for players that allows them to figure out where to go without being told *exactly* where to go. Moreover, getting in the light allows the player to see things more clearly.

LIFE OBSERVATION

How many of us go through life ostensibly in the light but actually are very much in the dark? Picture that second attacker described above; yes, she's in the game, technically part of the action, but in reality, she's just playing in the shadows of others. She's like a ship that doesn't want to leave the harbor – as the saying goes, she's safe but she's made for more. She needs a wake-up.

If we're honest I think most of us spend far too much time in the dark. To borrow a contemporary buzzword, we're present, but not *fully* present. Our heads are down, oblivious to the world. Ignorant of the real magic surrounding us, we keep our heads buried in our phones, staring at a computer screen, or watching TV. We are too often unwilling to look up as we remain stuck in our own little worlds.

This isn't a rant about modern technology; I am referring to more than that. I think social media is a symptom just as much as it is a cause. Much like the characters numbed by the drug Soma in Aldous Huxley's *Brave New World*, many of us seem to have lost the sense of wonder that little children have. We've chosen to withdraw from the brightness of the light and as a consequence we don't see things as they really are.

The world is an amazing place, but when we lose our curiosity, we miss *a lot,* and as a result, we find ourselves not as connected as we should be. Without the corresponding focus that accompanies our full engagement, it becomes virtually impossible to reach our full potential. In this simple scenario in a soccer game, the player doesn't have the awareness so she isn't asking herself how she can affect the game, or how she can help her teammates.

In reality, the human condition is somewhat predisposed to this; it becomes easy for most of us to grow comfortable and not fully participate in our own lives. At some point we find it easier to go through the motions rather than live as we should. Before we know it, we're spending too much of our lives in the shadows, and this extends to a diminishing focus and actions in school, our work, and even in our closest relationships. Rather than experience the highs and lows of living in the light, we may find ourselves in a constant state of gray.

When that happens, we need a reminder to get back in the light – to wake up to the wonders of the people and world around us. In the brightness of the day, we see things more clearly.

In a soccer game, when a player steps out of the shadows and into the light, she immediately inserts herself more effectively into the game. She opens herself up to the joys of fully participating and really playing the game. "Get in the light" is a good reminder for all of us – regardless of age.

"The world will never starve for want of wonders; but only for want of wonder." – GK Chesterton, English author and philosopher

Chapter 5

PLAY TO FEET

———— ⚽ ————

Getting the details right

"There's only one moment in which you can arrive in time. If you're not there, you're either too early or too late." – Johann Cruyff, legendary Dutch player and coach

"To feet!" It's a common instruction (though usually after a pass did *not* go to a player's feet). This reaction follows two different scenarios; either a ball was played where the passer expected a run from his teammate, or in some cases it was simply a bad pass that didn't find the intended target. The first deals with tactics, the second deals with technique. While the second one is a reminder about the need for better execution, the first is about understanding.

GAME SCENARIO

Playing to feet is a vital part of the game, especially when a team has the ball and is trying to keep possession in their defensive third. Passes to feet simply refer to a (usually short) pass directly to a player's feet, a pass so efficient that the player does not need to move a step or two to his right or left, but rather the ball gets to him where he wants it. At the higher levels it refers to not simply a pass to the player generally, but actually to the particular foot that allows the receiver to make the next play.

This doesn't mean that players are stationary; on the contrary, players constantly move off the ball to give themselves enough space in order to be available to receive a pass (as in every other arena in life, you don't want to be caught standing still). On a soccer field, it's easy to mark an immobile player; he wouldn't be considered much of a threat.

This movement by players "off the ball" needs to be intelligent. Players must constantly decide when and where to run to be in the right place at exactly the right time. I've mentioned this before, but it's also absolutely critical that the receiver knows what he's going to do with the ball before he gets it. Playing to feet in tight areas requires simple passes executed at speed – often with just one or two touches – and you can't have a series of quick interchanges if you don't know what you're going to do next.

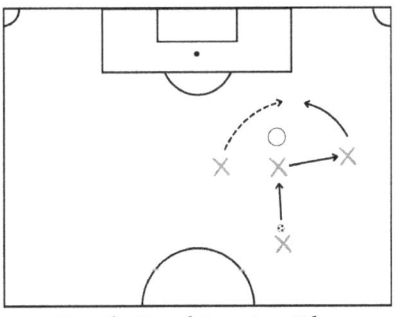

Quick Combination Play

When a ball is played to feet it is often because the receiver is tightly marked, and in general the space the team has to play in is small and congested. Given the need to be safe with the ball in the defensive third, a team typically does not want to play the ball into space as a high pressing team will have a better chance to intercept the ball close to goal. A team that has the technical competence and the tactical understanding to play its way out of its defensive third will be able to play to feet consistently.

It's an effective tool that gives players options. Based on the pass, the receiver can either turn or play the ball the way he is facing. Playing to feet involves quick passes and sudden, short bursts of players into space.

Playing to feet requires small, quick movements off the ball. Each player must consider the passing patterns as they develop and find space accordingly. Players need to think about not just the next pass, but a few moves ahead in order to help their teammates keep possession.

LIFE OBSERVATION

Something that appears simple is actually quite complex. Keeping possession consists of several small actions executed well and in harmony with others, all with active opposition. Done well, it looks easy, even though it really isn't. It takes hours of practice and work to get it right. It's a good metaphor for life. As adults, we know that anything worthwhile requires significant effort and sacrifice.

Kids don't necessarily get this. A high schooler, knowing he has a test in a week, might decide to wait to study for it until the night before (to disastrous results). Another example – maybe a student waits till the last minute to start a report – and doesn't do as well as he could have if he had put more effort in (and started sooner).

It's been said that carpentry is doing a lot of simple things correctly. A carpenter building something takes his time, ensuring that he gets all the small details right. When he's finished, he can be proud of his creation, satisfied with the care he put into the project.

Playing to feet in order to keep possession – successfully interchanging passes – is all about getting the fine details right. It's important for kids to learn that if something is worth doing, then it's worth paying attention to the details and getting it right.

"Details make perfection, and perfection is not a detail." – Leonardo Da Vinci

Chapter 6

PLAY TO SPACE

Taking advantage of opportunities

"I like to be active in space in behind the opposition's midfield.
That's where I can hurt the opponent most of all." – Thomas Muller

In the previous chapters we focused on staying connected and playing to feet. Often in the attacking third, it's also necessary to play to
"space," or send a ball into an open area where a teammate can run onto
the ball. Below is a diagram outlining the soccer field divided into thirds.
Players eventually learn the potential risks and advantages of actions in
each area of the field.

Soccer Field Divided into Thirds

At the younger ages, a simple instruction from a coach may be something
like the following: "If your teammate is open, pass to feet; if your teammate
is marked, pass to space." It is up to both players to recognize the triggers
so that they both know where the ball needs to go. In this way they have
the necessary head start on the defender.

GAME SCENARIO

In this situation the central midfielder sees a winger on the touchline closely marked by the outside defender. The central defender has not moved in that direction and there is plenty of space for a through ball that splits those defenders and allows the winger to run into a dangerous area to receive the ball.

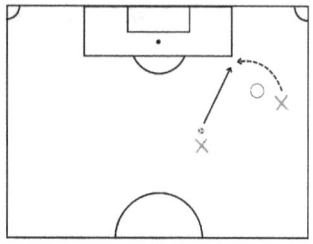

Through ball from center
midfielder to winger

At younger ages many coaches might instruct players to play "man to man," as this is a common tactic in other sports. In soccer, though, defending man to man in open play is a really difficult proposition. The field is so big; if a team is your equal technically or athletically, you're likely in for a hard time. At any point, if one player is beaten 1v1, you're in trouble, as space will be created all over the field. Dragging players out of good defensive positions is a relatively simple thing. If a winger puts her heels on the touchline, she opens up all sorts of space in the middle of the field – particularly if a defender stays close to her.

In this scenario, if the central defenders are occupied with opposing forwards, the outside defender is stranded. If the winger is but a foot faster, she'll have the easy advantage on a good through ball.

Players and coaches look for these advantages all over the field. Where is the space that we can create? How can we create it? What do we do when we find it?

During the course of a game, it often takes a long time to create space; good first touches, short passes, and smart runs often provide the opportunity to open up the field. That space becomes the window of opportunity that allows us to try something – but we have to see it and recognize it when it happens. Often, when it does, it's magic.

Finding the ball in open space is freedom. Receiving the ball when there are no defenders around is an exhilarating feeling. Getting on the end of a pass in space yields opportunities that didn't exist just a few moments prior. All of a sudden, the field opens up, and so do the options. A player can dribble, find a pass she likes, or simply take a shot.

The team has worked hard to create this chance. Diligently keeping the ball while under pressure, they saw the moment to take the advantage, and they took it. They bided their time until they saw the opportunity.

LIFE OBSERVATION

How often do we get so bogged down in what we're doing that we stop looking for the opportunity to take the next step? During a soccer game, those windows of opportunities are narrow. Especially against an organized defense, finding the spaces to attack can be challenging. When the window opens – however briefly – it's important to take a chance. Soccer teams train to look for those chances; it's a good lesson to learn off the field as well.

All too often in life it can seem like we're running on a hamster wheel. It's easy to see what we do as drudgery, and we can get locked into a monotonous cycle, where we stop searching for the next door to try.

We have to be on the lookout for opportunities, and when we find them, we have to be willing to take them. In this scenario, playing a "through ball" is not necessarily easy; there's a chance the pass could be intercepted. The key though, is the willingness to try. Players must foster the mindset that decides to give it a go.

This is what happens to us in life. We set goals and commit ourselves to smaller activities that bring us closer to our goals. Coupled with awareness, those good habits that we cultivate will, over time, open doors to opportunities we need to follow. When those opportunities do arise, we need to take advantage and be willing to grow.

"Our lives are defined by opportunities. Even the ones we miss." – Eric Roth, screenwriter for the film The Curious Case of Benjamin Button, based on the story by F. Scott Fitzgerald

Chapter 7

HEELS ON THE TOUCHLINE

—————— ⚽ ——————

Seeing things from a different perspective

"Chaos is merely order waiting to be deciphered." – José Saramago, Portuguese winner of the Nobel Prize in Literature

S pacing is such a critical component of the game. The positioning of players in relation to one another is obviously an essential part of this concept. Players off the ball need to situate themselves so that they can assist their teammate with the ball while giving that player room to operate.

GAME SCENARIO

Young players naturally gravitate towards the ball; this is perfectly normal. As they get older and the field becomes bigger they learn that it is more and more important to make as much space as possible. As players adjust to larger dimensions, wide players often gradually drift inside in the hopes of getting the ball. This is when you might hear the coach say, "Heels on the touchline." It's a simple reminder for the wide player to remain outside, creating as much space as possible.

This can be difficult for young players, and it does take some time for them to understand the value of doing this. Maintaining width is invaluable when trying to play possession. For a young player, it might seem like you're being outcast to a spot on the field where you're not involved in the game. Being put on the outside when all the action seems to be happening in the middle can be a little frustrating to a kid's mind.

We mentioned earlier how really young players are naturally self-focused. As kids mature, they grow in understanding about the importance of playing with others, sharing the ball, and the need to focus more on the team. On any team in any sport, players have roles to play, and the role of the wide player is essential to a soccer team.

A winger remaining out wide with his heels on the touchline provides an attacking outlet. Balls sprayed out to these players from the middle force the defense to adjust their spacing and opens up avenues for dribbling, give-and-goes, or through balls. Taken literally, putting your heels on the touchline is more than just positioning; it's also about orientation.

Winger receiving the ball with heels on the touchline

If your heels are on the touchline, you are facing the middle of the field, and consequently you have options when you receive the ball. You can pass or dribble backwards, towards the middle, or play the ball forward along the touchline. Your physical disposition offers the team more space, and your bodily orientation also prepares you for the next action because you have given yourself options.

Often coaches will put younger players in wide positions against older players, even if the coach projects the player to be a future center mid. Out wide, a player can see the game easier and will have more time to make decisions, away from what can be the hurly-burly of the midfield.

When a soccer player has his heels on the touchline the field opens up for him and he can see the whole game from where he stands. If he is observant and is thinking ahead, the game becomes easier because he can see and determine what should happen next when he gets the ball. Far from being out of the picture, he has gained the advantage because he can see both opportunities and threats.

Further, his physical stance will affect his attitude. Some players will get frustrated when they feel they don't get the ball enough. If his posture is lazy and unfocused, he will not be prepared to help his team when he does get the ball. This is generally a mark of player maturity. Even if he doesn't get the ball, he understands that he can help his teammates because from a wide position he sees things they can't. Because he can see the whole field, he can communicate to his team about where the ball should go next.

LIFE OBSERVATION

Life looks different from other vantage points, and while this seems obvious it can be easy to forget. What we *choose* to see matters. Our vantage point – our own field of vision – guides what we see, and sometimes from where we stand we are unable to see the whole picture. We have to remember that when our field of vision is limited, so is our understanding, which often means our sense of the reality of a situation is distorted.

Just as a winger must orient himself properly so that he sees as much of the field as possible, off the field we must recognize that if our vision of something is limited, we may have to change our perspective to see more clearly.

People often find it difficult to solve problems because (for whatever reason) they are unable to see the whole picture. Their view is incomplete and consequently they can't understand how to find the best solution. If you can't see it, you can't even identify the problem to solve. (Even simpler: if you can't see it, you can't solve it). Recognizing the problem for what it really is – that's the first step in solving it.

Whether it's a rumor at school that has spread like wildfire with no one questioning the premise, or a challenge at work that seems insurmountable, our vantage point matters. How much we see matters. If we can orient ourselves so that we can view the whole picture, we'll have a better chance of recognizing the situation for what it really is in order to find a good solution.

If, on the other hand, we refuse to see the whole challenge, we'll never solve the problem. Recognizing this involves some humility, because it requires an acceptance that, you know what – we don't know everything. Consequently, even attempting to change our perspective and see the fuller picture indicates that we're actively seeking to solve a problem. In a soccer game, heeding the advice of a coach to stay wide is a simple act of humility, and one that gives an advantage if it is embraced.

As we grow older, it becomes easier to recognize that we need to see more, because the truth is that it's difficult to know what to do next if you can't (or won't) see a problem in all its complexity. Seeing the whole problem enables you to plan, not just in the long-term, but simply to take the first step to solve it.

Young players will often "play with blinders on," and gravitate towards the ball even though that may not be their role. They focus on themselves and consequently limit their field of vision. It's understandable, because their natural inclination is to move towards the thing they want to play with. As they mature, they realize this is short-sighted, because they are missing an opportunity to be in a position where they can see so much more and help the team by being a more important part of the solution.

Still, how often do we as adults live with our "blinders" on? It takes courage to move out of our limited field of vision and see the bigger picture, but it's worth it, because only then will we be able to really see the problem and work toward a solution, even if it takes us out of our comfort zone.

It can be easy for people to get wrapped up in their own little worlds and not see the big picture. They're not willing to accept that there might be more to the story than what they can see from their limited worldview. To blame this on ignorance is too simplistic, because to some extent this is human nature; we may be naturally defensive, or we want to feel safe and in order to do that we sometimes look inward rather than outwards.

It takes courage to step out and be willing to open ourselves to a wider perspective. From overcoming stereotypes to navigating relationships, our viewpoint is critical. Simply seeking to understand another person's point of view or solving a problem – it all depends on our orientation.

"It is a narrow mind which cannot look at a subject from various points of view." – George Eliot, English novelist and poet

Chapter 8

KNOW WHAT TO DO WITH THE BALL
BEFORE YOU GET IT

———— ⚽ ————

Planning ahead to breed confidence

"Football is played with the head. Your feet are just the tools." –
Andrea Pirlo, Italian midfielder and World Cup winner

This one is a command that every soccer coach preaches to their players over and over again. It's not something you'll hear during a game, but it's a phrase coaches will hammer home all the time during practices and on the touchline during games.

It's self-explanatory; "Know what you're going to do with the ball before you get it." It certainly seems like common sense, something so basic that you wouldn't think needs to be explained. Yet some players never figure this out, and it shows when they play.

Knowledge in any arena is important. In a soccer game, knowing something your opponent doesn't gives you an advantage, and it breeds confidence. Players who are confident are able to really enjoy playing the game and are more likely to relax and be brave on the ball.

It's such a simple saying, yet like many simple things, beneath the surface it is quite complex. Let's take an example from the field.

GAME SCENARIO

There are dozens of situations to consider, but here's a simple one. Let's say you're a right back whose goalkeeper has the ball and intends to play out of the back through her defense. You have moved wide to create space, and your heels are on the touchline while you face the field. You put yourself in this position so that you will have options if and when you receive the ball. Standing on the half-turn allows you to play in multiple directions. If the goalkeeper or central defender plays you the ball and you are facing your own goal with opponents putting you under pressure, your only real option is to play the ball back to them. This is a problem because you have limited your team's ability to play out.

We discussed this in a previous chapter, but it bears repeating. Facing the middle of the field allows you to play the ball back, but also to the middle towards a central midfielder, or forward to a winger or striker. Continually surveying what's around you allows you to make the right choice, while the positioning gives you options. Which of your teammates are open? Who can make the next best play? Where does your team have an advantage in numbers? Is there space for you to dribble? Can you take the ball with one touch and beat a defender? These are just a few things a player must think about *before* the ball ever gets to her.

No matter where you are on the field, and regardless of where the ball is, you need to understand what you can and should do with the ball if it is played to you. It's not that you think about it only when it's approaching you; it's that you are aware at all times, so you can have a solution ready regardless of the situation. Your head is "on a swivel," taking in what is around you (teammates, opponents, spacing, etc.). When you see professional players play a one-touch pass, it's because they had taken several mental "snapshots" prior to receiving the ball as they are constantly surveying the scene around them.

The extent to which kids get this concept is a good indicator as to their "coachability." This level of awareness is what allows kids who aren't necessarily the most naturally athletic to still play at a high level. The professional model of this might be Sergio Busquets of Spain, who rarely (if ever) loses the ball. To look at him, you see a tall, gangly player, but his sublime touch and decision-making are unparalleled in the game.

LIFE OBSERVATION

We talked about awareness before. To know what you're going to do with the ball before you get it is to think ahead; to be aware of your surroundings in order to execute the best decision you can. I've heard it said that professionals routinely think 3-4 moves ahead. Players at every level must be thinking about what will happen next, and what their role in that movement is.

Like anything in life, thinking and planning ahead is critical to succeeding in any endeavor. The mental exercise of calculating in your head – of thinking through the possibilities, advantages, and potential pitfalls – enables you to make the best decision possible.

This forethought is essential. Without it, in a soccer game a player is likely to treat the ball as a hot potato, consequently finding herself unable to control the ball and keep possession for her team. Conversely, thinking ahead gives you options. By understanding the situation and surveying possibilities, a player can determine the best way forward.

Not to state the obvious, but not every plan is perfect. In a soccer game, there are so many scenarios and variables a player must consider. For example, you may hope to receive the ball on the ground, but what if you must deal with a bouncing ball that is hard to control while under defensive pressure?

You may not have planned for this, but the fact that you had been thinking through different scenarios in advance gives you some flexibility. Your first choice may be unavailable, but because you were aware of your surroundings and thought through the options, you are more likely to find a solution that works.

It goes without saying that this tool is needed in life. As kids mature, they are able to do more things. This is both good and bad. Yes, they can take on more responsibilities, but they are also capable of getting into trouble.

A common piece of advice to teenagers as the weekend begins is the simple phrase, "Make good decisions." That's a lot easier to do when you think through the consequences of an action in advance. Even better is having the awareness to put yourself in situations that lead to better choices.

An important part of awareness is preparation. In soccer, mastery of techniques, when combined with a solid assessment of one's surroundings, is what gives a player options. This combination of field awareness, ball mastery, and the options this provides gives a player confidence.

It's safe to say that everyone at some point has found themselves in a situation where they were caught flatfooted, maybe stumped by a question they weren't expecting, for example. It happens. But it is possible to prepare by thinking ahead, understanding what may come, and so plan for contingencies. This provides a huge confidence booster.

It's like the old saying, "I know something you don't." When you hear someone say it, the words come out as if they were dripping with confidence. It reveals a secret knowledge; an attacking player who knows what she's going to do has a big advantage over her opponent. And that edge gives a player the confidence to act.

Confidence is important for everyone, and sometimes a little mental preparation is all you need to ensure you're one step ahead of the game, safe in the knowledge that you understand what to do next.

"Luck is what happens when preparation meets opportunity." – *Seneca, Stoic philosopher*

Chapter 9

DON'T RUN AWAY

———————— ⚽ ————————

The importance of relationships

"In most scenarios it isn't the man on the ball who decides where the ball goes, but players without the ball. Their running actions determine the next pass." – Johann Cruyff

In all sports, vision, communication, and teamwork are critical, as the players are constantly trying to find open spaces to move the ball through. In soccer, if you make a blind turn or pass, you could run into a brick wall of a defender. The German philosopher Friedrich Nietzsche once said, "My idea of paradise is a straight line to goal." Well, we all recognize that most paths we have to take in our lives are not, in fact, straight lines. Instead, they're filled with all sorts of twists and turns and changes in direction. Soccer is much the same. A team has to move the ball multiple directions to clear a space to move the ball forward.

GAME SCENARIO

The following illustration demonstrates a common scenario referred to as "Up, Back, & Through." Here a midfielder plays the ball into a target forward, who rather than attempt a turn with a defender on his back, lays the ball off to another midfielder. As the ball is played backwards a wide forward further up the pitch recognizes the situation and begins a run towards goal. The second midfielder, who called for the ball and can see what is happening, plays a straight vertical ball forward for the diagonal run. The ball goes up, back, and through the defense.

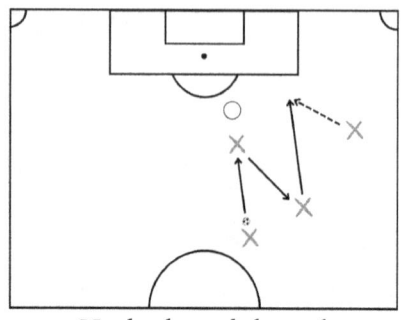

Up, back, and through

The instruction (verbal cue) in this situation is typically, "MAN ON!" This tells the receiver that an opponent is either right behind him waiting to pounce or is rapidly closing him down. If he hasn't checked his shoulders and doesn't know what is behind him, he needs to *trust* his teammate and return the ball to the sender or to another player he sees is unmarked. The player making the call can see the way forward and understands which path is most prudent.

Defenders must always be aware of the ball. If done fast and sharply, these simple passes force the defenders to adjust their positions. Moving the ball quickly moves the opposition and opens space to play forward. While it would be nice to be able to go straight to the goal we set for ourselves, we need to be able to adjust and change directions.

The trouble is that you don't necessarily see this in youth games. Often, especially in youth games, you can see a team trying to play out of the back with its defenders and midfielders passing to each other. While the next logical step should be to bring in the forwards (as illustrated above), immature players will miss the opportunity to connect.

All too often young forwards will take off on a sprint to get behind the defense, expecting a defender or midfielder to launch the ball up the field.

This is a common tactic, and you'll hear parents yell, "Hit it to the corner flag!!" This tactic always annoyed me, and when it is taught to kids at young ages, they often never really learn to do anything else. I've seen kids who play that ball to the corner (partly because they're just excited they can kick it that far) when they're 9 or 10, and when you see them in high school they're still doing the *same exact thing* – even when there are much better options available.

There are certainly times to play the ball into space, but that ball you see sent into the corner flag is a personal pet peeve. I mean, it's an inanimate object. It's not your teammate, and it certainly isn't going to pass the ball to you – yet you see it in almost every youth game you watch.

When young forwards take off (rather than coming back to the ball to participate in a team's possession build-up), they are leaving their teammate with the ball to fend for himself. At that point the player with the ball may be forced to pass laterally or behind him or may, as a last resort, end up simply knocking the ball long and just...hoping.

What had been an opportunity for his team to keep possession becomes at best a 50-50 ball (but more likely a turnover). This is when you may hear, "DON'T RUN AWAY!" from a coach who wants his team to keep the ball. Coaches want their teams to stay connected on the field. As players get older and tactics become more advanced, the importance of positioning and proper spacing can't be overstated.

As kids get older and learn to play with more teammates, a basic priority is the connections, that is, the relationships players have with nearby teammates. During a game, how they communicate and play off each other becomes really important. Players must develop an understanding of how to play and work together for the good of the team.

Let's take a look at one position and consider a few possible connections:

- Right Back connected with the Right Wing;

- Right Back connected with the CenterBacks;

- Right Back connected with the Center Defensive Midfielder

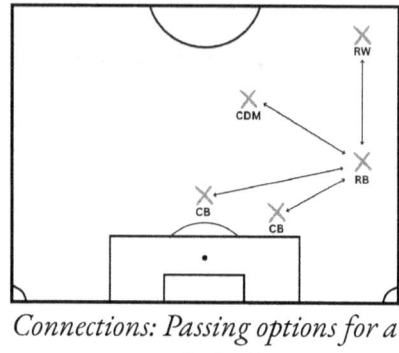

Connections: Passing options for a right back

Obviously, there are more options, but these three connections are paramount because they are the closest teammates and represent the primary relationships for a right back. Even though the field gets bigger as kids get older, the basic rule remains the same; the closest relationships remain the most important, which is why staying connected is critical. You help your teammates grow and they do the same for you. The whole team gets better as you learn how your playing styles mesh together. This is the same in life; at a young age, kids develop relationships with their neighbors and classmates. They learn to play and work together, developing a fluency as they grow.

LIFE OBSERVATION

If you think about it, making and improving connections is how we humans develop. We are social animals, hard-wired to interact with our environment. To think, we learn to "put two and two together," to make connections in order to figure out how to solve problems. We begin to see how people and things are interrelated. We grow emotionally and spiritually by learning from others and communicating so we can understand and be understood, and we come to realize that we can achieve more as a group than as individuals.

Good training sessions include activities that allow these connections to grow in a variety of situations. The more the group works together, the quicker they will be able to respond to problems on the field as a unit.

We know innately that developing relationships is essential – but we also know that personal connections with other people only improve when people spend time together and take the time to communicate and learn from each other. Good relationships require consistent communication and work. When we lose touch with people, these connections begin to fray.

As kids get older, the world they live in gets larger. On a soccer field, as players mature their connections necessarily grow wider. While the right back needs to retain those early relationships listed above, on a bigger field with more teammates those connections will extend to the Center Attacking Midfielder, the Forward, and ultimately the rest of the team.

In this illustration, enhancing the connections between players allows a team to play well in tight spaces rather than merely launch the ball forward to the corner flag. By connecting the forward to the rest of the group, the whole team has the opportunity to move as a unit, enabling them to stay united. When that forward runs away, he is effectively leaving the team disjointed. Ultimately, the attack will likely fail, and the other team will win the ball. The temptation for a striker to get forward is understandable, but we shouldn't want to run away from our friends if we want the group to stay together and succeed.

We adults know that maintaining close relationships isn't easy; in fact, it requires a lot of work, and often is not something we feel like doing. It's important to remember, though, that the connections we forge impact us throughout our lives, and because we are made for each other, ultimately our well-being is dependent upon our efforts to maintain them and make new ones.

"A real friend is one who walks in when the rest of the world walks out." – Walter Winchell, American columnist

Chapter 10

KEEP IT

———————— ⚽ ————————

Controlling how we respond to challenges

"There is only one ball, so you must have it." – Johann Cruyff

E veryone has heard the phrase, "The best defense is a good offense." This applies also to soccer. The game is continuous, and what kids are taught from a very young age is that while yes, some players are labeled "defenders," or "forwards," all players on the field are attackers when their team has the ball, and defenders when they don't (and for those youth parents out there who get nervous when somebody passes the ball back to the goalkeeper, yes this includes the keeper).

GAME SCENARIO

It is vitally important that young kids learn how to play a possession style, perhaps most importantly because it provides the best pattern of development (any athletic kid can learn how to play "Route 1" (whereby the ball is played long in the air from the defense to the forward, essentially bypassing the midfield), but the development of technical and tactical skills are forged in a possession environment).

Like any sport, soccer tactics are always evolving. Styles of play come in and out of prominence. In the mid-2000s the world was enraptured by watching Spain and Barcelona dominate world football with a possession-oriented attacking style. The manner in which these teams played meant that, counter-intuitively, their possession style formed a sort of defense. Having the ball 60-70% of the game meant that well... their opponents didn't. Further, because they utilized a lot of short passes, when they would lose the ball, players were connected closely together so they could all press in unison and essentially suffocate the ball winner, getting the ball back quickly and beginning the attacking process all over again.

To the untrained eye, the short passes inherent in such a style might seem pointless, as if the team with the ball is just passing it around aimlessly amongst themselves with no purpose. Here it's important to remember that every movement of the ball should serve to somehow unlock the opposition. Think of chess; initial movements of the pawns may seem inconsequential, but the opponent must consider what opportunities lie on the board now that space is created for other pieces.

Sometimes, especially against an organized defense, finding those opportunities takes time (scoring goals isn't easy!). Especially for young players, when a team is attacking, a coach may get a sense that the players are getting impatient, about to make a decision that will not likely lead to a goal (e.g., *forced* shot from a bad angle; *forced* dribble into a congested area; *forced* longer pass with little chance of finding its target; etc.). At that point, she may yell, "KEEP IT!" to remind her players they can always play backwards and that they don't have to go forward all the time. This can be a challenge for young players, but over time they realize the best teams are comfortable with recycling the ball through their defenders and midfielders until they find the best opportunity to create a good chance. The point is to connect with your teammates, find an open player, and keep the play simple. I don't mean to belabor the point, but by refusing to be forced into a bad decision, players can effectively control the game. Regardless of what the opposition does, when you have the ball, you are in control, so it's important to resist those impulses to force something that probably won't work.

Young players may not realize it at the moment, but there's a simple principle in play here; keeping the ball is vital because if you have it, the opponent can't score. Initially it may seem as if the scoring chances aren't coming, but on the flipside, for soccer players it's very frustrating when your team can't seem to get a hold of the ball, and all you're doing is running after it. For teams that are good at keeping the ball, the game is more fun. All the players are involved, moving and creating space for each other. There is a psychological benefit of playing this way as well, because when you have the ball, you enjoy the game more and don't feel tired. Playing with the ball fosters a sense of control, which enables a team to effectively dictate when to attack.

LIFE OBSERVATION

To "keep it" means to pass away from danger, buy some time and regroup, and think about a better option, and this requires patience. In order to maintain control, patience and fortitude are needed to prevent making a hasty decision that will lose the ball.

Let's face it; we are all impatient at times. Sometimes we run into situations headlong without really thinking of the consequences, whether in school, at work, or in relationships. Sometimes we say things we shouldn't (or at least things we haven't really thought through first) and the result is that we end up losing control. Times like these are when we should try to "keep it;" keep it together if you will. There are plenty of things that happen in life to frustrate us, make us angry, or even cause us to lash out at someone.

Sometimes when we're trying to do something, inevitably a monkey wrench gets thrown into our plans, and it can be really frustrating. When this happens, emotions can take over if we're not careful. Disruptions in our lives, things outside of our control, happen all the time. Even the best laid plans can sometimes run amok, regardless of our efforts.

While we can't control these disruptions, we can control how we respond to them. By maintaining control of our emotions, we can respond in a clearer way, giving ourselves a better chance of getting the outcome we want.

In terms of soccer, the opponent will do whatever it can to steal the ball. But if you can keep it, you maintain control of the situation. In soccer we can control the ball. In life, we can control our emotions. By controlling our emotions in response to something negative (instead of lashing out angrily, for example), we remain in command. This isn't to say the emotions aren't there, rather that controlling our response sets us up for a successful resolution. Everyone lashes out at some point, but the critical thing is to understand that it is our *response* to a situation (not the situation itself) that is under our control.

Whether it's a setback in school or work (e.g., a bad grade, or a rejection from the college we wanted to go to), these things happen to everyone and how we respond to it is much more important than the event itself. There are always other options available, and by taking a step back and remaining in control we can examine the challenge from a broader perspective. Doing so often lets us see the solution we've been looking for.

"Everything can be taken from a man but one thing: the last of the human freedoms - to choose one's attitude in any given set of circumstances, to choose one's own way." – Viktor Frankl, Austrian neurologist, philosopher, and Holocaust survivor

Chapter 11

KEEP IT MOVING

———— ⚽ ————

Purpose guides decisions

"We do not pass to move the ball; we pass to move the opposition."
– Pep Guardiola

Sometimes the game slows down. When you're in possession, it's important to be looking for ways to break down the opposition as defenses naturally react to the movement of the ball.

Remember that every movement of the ball should serve to somehow unlock the opposition.

In soccer, every defense likes slow, predictable ball movement. If a team in possession fails to move the ball quickly, it's easier for the defense to stay compact and ultimately force a mistake. If the attacking team is unable to move the ball out of a tight situation and open up the field, the defense will be able to apply pressure and effectively collapse the space around the ball, forcing a turnover. Every time the ball moves, the defense as a team must react and move in relation to the ball...so logically, the quicker the ball movement, the better.

Passing the ball just for the sake of passing isn't what we're talking about. It may seem counterintuitive, but lateral and negative passes help a team keep possession and probe for an opening. Attacking support off the ball, with teammates taking up good positions as a collective unit, allows for sustained possession and ultimately, attacking opportunities.

GAME SCENARIO

Good teams use precise, one-touch passes to move the ball quickly and force the opponent to change positions. When executed well, these coordinated passing patterns are a joy to behold. Short, sharp player movements off the ball provide a team with passing options in multiple directions and leave the opponent struggling for answers. Prolonged passing sequences develop a rhythm as the ball is given and received like clockwork, as if an invisible metronome was providing the beat in the background.

This intelligent ball movement enables a team to control the game while biding its time as it probes for an opening. Teams that become proficient at this are always on the lookout for triggers from the opponent that signal when an attack should occur. Such a trigger might be a 1v1 situation close to goal, or an advantage in numbers on one side of the field where there is no defensive support. Regardless, the key is finding the right moment to attack and seize the opportunity.

While the team is passing the ball, each player is looking for those cues to attack, and keeping the ball moving quickly allows players to search for those moments while maintaining control. On occasions when the play slows down the coach may encourage his team with a reminder to "Keep it moving," to wear the opponent down by forcing them to adjust to quicker changes of direction.

The idea behind this command is about reinforcing the idea of *purpose*. All teams work at keeping the ball, but the point of possession is to translate that control into goals. I've seen plenty of teams that can keep the ball for long periods but have no idea how to do the most fundamental thing in soccer (score goals).

As stated in the previous chapter, possession offers control, which is important, but only one part of the equation. The key is to use that control to get what you want (in this case, to score a goal). "Keep it moving" reminds players why they're there. It's a direction that carries a bit of urgency, a command to players to actively seek out opportunities to go to goal.

Sometimes in soccer, defenders knocking the ball around endlessly gives the illusion of control, but this is more akin to "busywork" rather than productivity. You could argue that a team is in control, but it has no use. Sometimes it can be easy to forget this. At some point, we've all gotten caught not seeing the forest for the trees. As humans we often get stuck in a rut of "busyness" and forget what we're trying to achieve! We may appear as if we're in control, but the reality is that we're just busy, and not really accomplishing anything important.

While keeping the ball is a strategic tool (demonstrating control, patience, and awareness), "Keep it moving" is an instruction to actively seek out the right moment to strike. The attitude of patience required by the team keeping the ball now becomes more proactive, as playing the ball quicker should create the openings we're looking for.

In order to find those opportunities, a good sense of timing is required to coordinate those fast, sharp off the ball movements we mentioned earlier.

"There is only one moment in which you can arrive in time. If you're not there, you're either too early or too late." - Johann Cruyff

There is a field of science known as cybernetics[1], which relates to the study of the relationship between control and communication related to achieving a goal (purpose). In a soccer game, control of a game could

---

1. Pangaro, Paul. "Getting Started Guide to Cybernetics," pangaro.com [http s://www.pangaro.com/definition-cybernetics.html].

be a team's possession of the ball, while communication relates to the quicker passing sequences and coordinated, active search for opportunities to attack the goal discussed here. Essentially, it's understanding a process to identify the correct timing for an action that will create a successful outcome. Why bring this up in a book about soccer?

Let's go back to the Barcelona example. At their peak they would keep the ball for long periods, gently probing while they waited for the right moment. At times it was as if they would lull the opponent to sleep, but suddenly an opening would appear thanks to their patience and with a quick give-and-go or 1v1 dribble, they would score a goal. As a team, the players observed how the opponent defended and modified their decisions accordingly. The players understood the correct moment to strike.

LIFE OBSERVATION

The patience it takes to wait for those moments (and the understanding required to notice and act on those moments) is something people develop as they mature. This is a skill that people use without knowing in all facets of their lives. The technical and tactical skills used to keep the ball help players recognize the moment to attack. Likewise, the good habits we develop as we build on our experiences in life while we work towards our goals prepare us to recognize and act when opportunities arise.

You may have heard the phrase, "Just do the next right thing." Moving forward, doing the proper thing in the next moment, this builds good habits, and these habits serve us well. Consistently making good decisions is the preparation that increases the likelihood of successfully seizing the opportunity when it comes. We will be able to recognize the moment because of how we trained ourselves. In the meantime, we "keep it moving."

Just a quick clarification, when I mention these "next" decisions, I'm not necessarily talking about big life decisions. I'm simply referring to whatever little choice lies in front of us. Making the next right choice is an easy way to stay on the right path. In a soccer game a player doesn't need to attempt a long dangerous ball; he can simply make a short pass to an open teammate. It's the same in life; just make the next right decision and move on from there.

The fact is, in soccer keeping the ball is hard; playing faster while maintaining control is even more difficult. Good teams make it look easy, since in many ways it's about doing the little things well, over and over again. As we get older, we come to realize that in life, sometimes the hardest thing we have to do is simply wake up every day to consistently meet our obligations, no matter how mundane they may be. It takes effort, love, persistence, and dedication (in the words of GK Chesterton, "Daybreak is a never-ending glory, getting out of bed is a never-ending nuisance.").

These tasks become easier, though, when we remember *why* we do them. The habits we develop over time reinforce our purpose and prepare us to make the right choice when confronted with a big decision.

The technical and tactical skills used to keep the ball help players to recognize the moment to attack the goal. Likewise, the good habits we develop as we build on our experiences in life as we work towards our goals prepare us to recognize and act when opportunities arise.

"Habits change into character." – Ovid, Roman poet

Chapter 12

TIME

———— ⚽ ————

Prioritize how to spend time

"Football is a wonderful and extremely wise game. The secret of football is time, space, and illusion. As in life, manage time, find space and be in control of the illusion." – Cesar Luis Menotti, Argentinian player and manager

Speed of play is everything in soccer. How quickly a team can move the ball while maintaining control is indicative of their level of play. That said (though you might not know it from watching much youth soccer), the game is not supposed to be played at 90 miles per hour all the time. There is a natural ebb and flow to the game.

Think of the size of the field and the length of a game. At the professional level, the field can be up to 120 x 80 yards and the game is 90 minutes. Players may run between 6 and 9 miles a game. We can't expect players to sprint for those 90 minutes, so players understand that there is a natural pace to the sport. There are times when the play is very fast, and other times the game seems to slow down.

When you watch some teams, it seems like their play is effortless. They aren't doing anything out of the ordinary, yet they move the ball very well. Their technique is excellent, and their understanding of space gives them that most precious ingredient – time.

Time and space are the basic elements of soccer. When your team is on the ball, time is the key ingredient. Time provides opportunity to find the answers needed to solve the problems presented by the opposition.

We all know that time is a precious commodity (though admittedly we waste a lot of it). On a soccer field, you'll hear this word often. "Time!" a teammate may yell to a player about to receive a pass, letting them know they are not under immediate pressure and can take the time to settle the ball and evaluate their options.

GAME SCENARIO

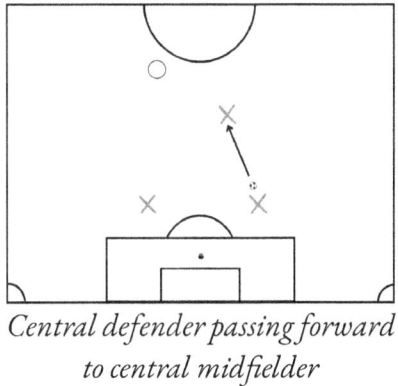

Central defender passing forward
to central midfielder

A simple example of this is when a central defender passes the ball forward to the central defensive mid and says, "Time." It relays the message that she can turn with the ball and consider where the ball should go next. From here this player can dictate the next phase of play.

Time – it's something everyone wants more of. Time to make decisions, time to do things, etc. It's the same with soccer. Players on the ball want more time to decide how best to help their team. The thing about time is that it tells the truth. In soccer, it reveals how good a player you are. Every player looks good when they have a lot of time on the ball. In the words of Johan Cruyff, "In a small space a player has to be able to act quickly. A

good player who needs too much time can suddenly become a bad player."
When space is limited and a player is under pressure because she doesn't
have time, her quality is revealed.

LIFE OBSERVATION

It's difficult to perform any task when you're under the clock. In a crowded
midfield it can be hard for a central defensive midfielder to receive a ball,
turn away from pressure, and keep possession while opponents are breathing down your neck. The best manage to do so and create time for their
team.

This begs the question, how do you "create" time? Amidst all the activities
pulling us this way and that way, how do we give ourselves more time for
what's important?

Today it seems like everyone wishes for more time. We are all stretched in
many directions, running from one thing to another with little time for
rest or leisure. Everything is hurried, and living our lives this way makes it
nearly impossible to focus well on any one thing. It's always about the *next*
thing, rather than being "present" in the here and now.

A good midfielder, while thinking ahead, must be completely focused on
the present and move into the space that gives her the time she needs.

It's telling that a cottage industry of "experts" exists who can help people
and organizations streamline what they do and focus on important things.
Time is what it is; it's a constant that we can't change. That is, the idea that
we can "create" time is an illusion. What we can do, however, is use time
wisely. In a soccer game, both space and time are finite. Good teams, with
good movement off the ball, sharp passes and communication, create the
illusion of control.

A midfielder knows if she moves a few steps into space and receives a pass on the half-turn she'll be able to take a touch around an opponent and play a good ball. Moving into a small pocket of space will give her the time she needs. She's focused on the task at hand, not what she's going to do after the game. That laser-like focus allows her to think clearly.

She is both "present" in the moment and has her priorities in order. In a sense, for her time is irrelevant. She's "in the zone," as athletes call it. Nothing can distract her from her job.

Let's be clear, this laser-like focus is not something people can be expected to have 24/7. But by prioritizing our activities we can do better. If we're honest, I think most of us would acknowledge that some of our commitments (though worthwhile) may not be the best use of our time and have become more of a distraction. Eliminating them, and finding time for true leisure, would allow us to sharpen our focus on things that matter.

I don't want to go down a rabbit hole here but suffice it to say that leisure time has lost its meaning. The idea of leisure time should not mean sitting on the couch binge watching a tv series or doomscrolling on social media.

True leisure time also requires focus, enriching ourselves in an activity which helps us grow while our bodies rest and recover. Contrast doom scrolling with reading a good book. One negatively affects our ability to focus, while the other is enlightening.

Leisure time spent wisely increases our ability to concentrate in other areas of our lives.

I think most of us would be pretty happy if someone joyfully told us we had plenty of time for something. But then, what would we do with it? Would we spend that time wisely – or would we waste it?

Again, we all know instinctively that time is precious. We humans are born with special gifts, but do we use them? As I said before, time tells the truth; it reveals something. How we spend our time says something about us and what we value. A midfielder who is told she has time on the ball must use it wisely. Sometimes in a tight game those moments when a midfielder has the ball with time and space are few and far between. It's clear that these moments can't be wasted. She has to weigh her options and make the best decision she can for the good of the team.

Perhaps we can take a lesson from that midfielder. If she's focused and so engaged with what she's doing, she'll stand a decent chance of making the best decision for her team. With that magic ball at her feet, scanning the field for opportunities, she is really having a "zen" moment.

That's the way we should treat the time we have – that it's precious and not to be wasted.

"The common man is not concerned about the passage of time, the man of talent is driven by it." – Arthur Schopenhauer, German philosopher

Chapter 13

CARRY (TAKE YOUR SPACE)

———— ⚽ ————

Stepping outside your comfort zone

"You owe it to yourself to be the best you can be." – Christian Pulisic, American soccer player

L et's face it, everyone who plays soccer enjoys running with the ball, and when a defender gets the opportunity, he should take it. When that space opens up in front of you and you begin charging over that grass with the ball at your feet, it's a great feeling.

GAME SCENARIO

The ball has just been switched to the Right Back, where he is unmarked with plenty of room in front of him. His teammates yell to him, "TAKE YOUR SPACE!" and he moves forward with the ball. We spoke earlier of how important it is to move the ball in order to move the opposition, and dribbling is another method to do this.

By running at defenders, you force them to deal with you. Defending is all about managing space and time. Defenders like to keep everything in front of them, positioning themselves in order to control the game. Defenders have to decide how, when, and where to confront an attacker, and by running at them you force their hand and dictate the pace of the game.

This raid into space sets off a series of considerations. The defender carrying the ball forces the opponents to make a number of fast decisions.

By moving forward, he is asking questions of the opponents, who must try to come up with answers in a hurry (e.g., does the defense close down the attacker or do they drop a little deeper?). My purpose isn't to go into tactical nuance here, I just want to point out that by aggressively taking the space in front of him, the defender is forcing the issue and confidently taking the matter into his own hands.

While he is forcing the opponent into a decisive quandary, he needs to be thinking ahead as well. By taking the initiative, he has given his team an advantage so it's important that he quickly look at his options and figure out what to do next as he gallops up the field.

Some young players may take this space but end up dribbling into a blind alley and lose the ball. Others may pass too soon, and not really affect the opponent's defensive structure.

The key to remember when running at the defense is to force the defender to commit to you before passing the ball to a teammate. Doing this breaks a line of defense and forces the opponent to scramble to re-organize. This gives the attacking team some momentum and perhaps an opportunity to create a shot on goal.

LIFE OBSERVATION

It's important for us all to remember the important question, "What is the game asking?" At each moment in a game (and throughout our lives), we should all be asking ourselves this question. The right back mentioned above may be an introvert who doesn't like the spotlight. Maybe he is more comfortable with the defensive side of the game rather than the art of dribbling.

The point is that everyone is occasionally thrust into situations that seem far outside their comfort zone. Still, one thing we should encourage our kids to be is well-rounded. Kids should know and accept that there will be times in their lives when they'll have to do the unexpected. What life often requires of us can be quite surprising.

We may have to speak in public; we may have to write a report about something we don't really understand. We may be reserved and reluctant to argue with others but find ourselves forced to confront someone. *What is the game asking?* Young players gradually learn what they are called to do in certain situations, and their teammates rely on them to do it. As we grow, we learn what is expected of us in all areas of our lives. It's important to recognize what we are called to do and then have the bravery to actually do it.

"The sun himself is weak when he first rises, and gathers strength and courage as the day gets on." – Charles Dickens

Chapter 14

RELAX

—————— ⚽ ——————

Remaining calm in chaotic moments

"Before every kick of the ball there has to be a thought." – Dennis Bergkamp, Dutch soccer player

We mentioned before that kids love to dribble. The pure joy of having the ball at your feet...running with it, changing directions while everyone chases you around the field. It's fun!

But then we get older. At some point we transition from the idea that the world revolves around us to the understanding that there are other people in the world and it's important to take them into consideration when deciding on our actions. We move on (well, most of us) from that ego-centered world of the self, becoming more aware of others and how we affect each other. Our perception changes. Part of this concerns our thought process; we begin to imagine what other people think of us, and sometimes we allow these thoughts to affect our decisions.

We begin to face pressure (real or simply perceived) from others and ourselves. Ultimately this pressure can lead to a loss of confidence because we don't feel as free as we once were. We become more self-conscious, and as a result more restrained in our words and actions. In short, we fail to express ourselves fully because we are afraid of what others will think.

We may not realize it, but this can have dire consequences. In terms of sports, we might begin limiting ourselves, doing less than we used to; unwilling to try something new or adventurous. We stay "within ourselves," not doing what we should and ultimately, not becoming the best version of ourselves.

GAME SCENARIO

In a team setting, this manifests in different ways. We still focus on our own role but also become cognizant of how what we do affects our team as a whole. Sometimes, as kids get older, that joy of having a ball at your feet gives way to fear, fear of making a mistake and losing the ball, of letting your teammates and coaches down. In a soccer game, ultimately this fear leads to a desire to get rid of the ball...as quickly as possible!

When this happens, the ball (what was once a magical thing to be cherished) becomes more of a hot potato, bouncing from player to player, often aimlessly.

For coaches, this can be frustrating, especially since they know that it's not necessarily a question of skill; most athletes who have been playing the game for a period of time are capable of pulling off a few basic moves to get themselves out of trouble. The root cause is that player's concern about losing the ball and possibly hurting her team.

Fear affects the player's mindset, so let's take a minute and think about what that means. Fear distorts our vision. Fear manipulates our perception so that our vision of objective reality is distorted. In other words, when we're afraid, we don't see things as they really are, and this altered viewpoint affects how we respond to the world around us.

Sometimes when we're scared, we want to do something (anything!) to avoid confronting that emotion. When people are afraid, they respond in different ways. In sports, this avoidance can be disguised in how we play.

On a soccer field, some players who aren't comfortable on the ball in tight spaces, may instead play an uber-aggressive style, going in hard on physical challenges or kicking the ball a mile away. You could say this constitutes physical bravery, and it certainly does, but it may also be hiding a fear or lack of self-confidence. We have to get to the root of it; why is the player kicking the ball away instead of making a pass?

What happens all too often in youth soccer is that parents and coaches heap praise on the players who revel in the physical contest without considering that element's impact on the game. To make matters worse, they downplay the more technical players who can somehow dribble their way out of a phone booth. The reality is that these players represent another kind of bravery. They display a fortitude that comes from a willingness to restore order from chaos by "putting a foot on the ball" and finding a way out of tight spaces.

I can't tell you how many times I've witnessed a physically aggressive player charge through opponents like a bull in a china shop to thunderous applause from parents – only to give the ball away as soon as she'd won it. These parents miss the point; yes, her willingness to challenge for the ball is to be commended, but if all she does is kick it away, then what's the point? Coaches need to emphasize that overcoming the fear of losing the ball in a tough spot in order to maintain possession requires mental strength and bravery; those elements are not just reserved for players who fling themselves into a tackle.

Now I want to make it clear; the game is a home to all kinds of players in various shapes and sizes and that's part of what makes the game so universal. The trouble comes when we belittle or condemn the players who try to remain calm in a pressure situation and who try to keep the ball in tight spaces. This is the kind of bravery we want to nurture.

LIFE OBSERVATION

A game of soccer provides a perfect simulation of the chaos and pressures of life. This is why it's important to encourage young players to look at the pressure within the game and to understand that the best chance to succeed is to try to rise above the chaos and restore order.

The best coaches encourage players to see the challenges on the field as problems to be solved rather than battles to win. This is a better lens for young players to see the game. Headlong, aggressive challenges may win a brief battle on the field, but they won't be the solution in the long run. Staying calm and being able to keep the ball under pressure is the best platform for restoring order and taking control of the game.

Far too many youth soccer games devolve into that crazy game of hot potato. Players who can remain calm and find a solution where others can't are a great asset to any team because they essentially make it easier to control the game. Take it from Xavi, one of the finest midfielders of his generation: "Clearing the ball is an intellectual defeat: Can I not do anything else? When you recover the ball and lose it, you give possession to the opponent. Find spaces, pass to the goalkeeper, dribble, get a throw-in by shooting the ball off the player. Do something but do not kick it out!"

That kind of bravery (and sense of calm) is necessary in all areas of life. Consider the opening lines from the famous poem "If," by Rudyard Kipling, extolling what it takes to become a man:

"If you can keep your head when all about you are losing theirs and blaming it on you..."

Our goal as parents and coaches should be to foster that calmness, to develop young people who can keep their heads as the storm is raging around them. When the game is hectic, and the ball is rarely under control by either team, players start running around aimlessly. Yes, there's a flurry of activity, but how much of it is meaningful?

Remaining calm amidst such a swirl of activity offers a better chance to see things as they really are. This calmness fosters courage, because if we remember that fear is only a distortion of what's real, then as we can relax and get a clear image of what's happening, we are more likely to find a solution (something better than turning a soccer match into a game of kickball).

When you see a player in a tight space under pressure and you hear the coach yell, "RELAX!" you'll understand why.

All too often in life we equate activity with meaning. Watch any youth soccer game and you'll see players running around like chickens with their heads cut off. Yes, they're "busy," but is the movement meaningful? What is the intent behind all that activity?

Sometimes (even as adults) we find ourselves so "busy" that we are missing what's happening all around us. Pressure – even the perception of pressure – can affect how we do things. We fail to see the problem objectively. We struggle to "connect the dots" because we've lost sight of what's really happening. We've all been in situations where because of one or multiple misperceptions, people can't seem to see the forest for the trees. They overthink and overcomplicate things, rather than taking a step back and realizing that the simplest solution is often the best one.

Cultivating that sense of calm amid the storm is so important for young people to learn. On the soccer field, a way to do that might be as simple as executing a basic move like a pullback to find some space and play the ball backwards to keep possession.

In real life, it might mean biting your tongue rather than responding angrily to a verbal challenge. In such a situation, what if we were to take a breath and say, "You raise a really good point; let me get back to you on that."

The most effective leaders I've known were the ones who didn't snap or get angry in the face of a crisis. Instead, they maintained a calm demeanor and sought to fix the problem, not the blame.

"Stop trying to calm the storm. Calm yourself, the storm will pass."
– Buddha

Chapter 15

GO HOME

───── ⚽ ─────

Keeping options open

"In my teams, the goalie is the first attacker, and the striker is the first defender." – Johann Cruyff

Well, here's one for the older kids. What happens when they do finally start to "spread out" and recognize the space? Throughout these pages we've been highlighting the importance of possession-based soccer in terms of development. A big part of playing possession soccer involves the use of the goalkeeper in many passing sequences. In almost any situation, he can become an extra field player; an outlet for his teammates when they get caught in trouble.

GAME SCENARIO

All too often in most youth games we see players kick the ball "away" when they get in trouble. It's hard to blame them when the cacophony from the sidelines to "BOOT IT!" becomes overwhelming. The best coaches, however, teach the value of passing back to the 'keeper, as he usually has time and space to make a play that will allow the team to keep the ball.

Initially, this can be really challenging for parents ("Not that way!!"), but it really is the smart decision. Defenders who kick the ball out of bounds when they're chasing the ball and heading to their own goal are doing their teams a disservice. You have the opportunity to play the 'keeper and start another attack; don't give the ball away in your own defensive third!

Especially since the change in the pass-back rule in 1992, when goalkeepers were first required to use their feet when a teammate played the ball to them, goalkeepers have needed to evolve to have a certain competency with their feet. Prior to this change defenders could pass the ball to their keeper who could pick it up with his hands. This became a common tactic and it was decided that in order to speed the game up, 'keepers would not be able to pick up a ball; they would have to play it like any other field player.

It's hard to really overstate what that change was like (both tactically in how teams played) and how goalkeepers evolved. The best at using their feet become a sort of "sweeper-keeper," a player who plays behind the defense and helps retain possession even when under pressure.

This feature of the game is great for kids, as it's important for all players to learn these skills. While plenty of young players enjoy playing in goal, most don't want to do it for entire games. They want to kick the ball, and using them to maintain possession is a great way to keep them involved.

Simply, a defender under pressure plays the ball back to his keeper rather than kicking it out of bounds and ceding possession. Typically, the keeper receives it from one side and plays it to the other. So, if the left back has the ball and plays it to the keeper, the keeper takes a touch and maybe plays it to his right back. If the left back is under pressure, the right back will move as wide as he can and get in space as soon as the ball is played to the keeper. The keeper plays it to the right back and effectively switches the point of attack.

Left back to goalkeeper to right back

Rather than yell, "NOT TO THE KEEPER!" parents should understand that this is the smart play. In the modern era, most professional teams try to play out of the back, and yes, sometimes mistakes happen, and a goal is conceded. This will happen in the youth game as well, but it's important to remember that this is normal in development. Yes, a youth team will concede goals, but it's not the World Cup. They can't learn if they don't try it.

LIFE OBSERVATION

Kicking the ball away is basically throwing away an opportunity. It's for-saking a prospect for short-term safety. We don't have to throw away an opportunity when problems surface. When we can't immediately solve a problem, we can still recognize that there is another way. Playing the ball safely to the keeper while searching for other solutions is perfectly acceptable. Again, it's about keeping long-term gain possible.

Over the last 20 years goalkeepers have effectively become true field players when their team is in possession. Because of their position in front of goal, they can serve as a pivot of the attack, spraying the ball to a teammate anywhere on the field. When they do receive the ball, they typically have the most time and space to pick out a pass, serving essentially as a safety valve for defenders under pressure. Out in the real world, we often have more solutions available to us than we think, even if we're in a situation when we're seemingly under enormous pressure. When we can remain calm and remember our surroundings, we have a better chance of figuring it out. This also requires preparation; knowing what's available to us before we find ourselves in trouble can make all the difference. Just as a team would practice working with a keeper to play out of the back, it is important to be prepared to understand how to find a different kind of outlet than we generally might.

In soccer, I never understood teams who refused to use the goalkeeper to keep the ball. I've seen too many youth teams whose defenders would rather kick the ball away than pass to their own teammate in goal.

It just doesn't make much sense. When you're in a tough situation, you want to have all possible options available to you. Ignoring the goalkeeper is like throwing away a lifeline. At best you're just wasting resources. It may be hard to remember but the game is 11v11, not 10v11. Refusing to use your goalkeeper when appropriate is essentially playing at a disadvantage.

There are times in life when maybe sooner or later we need some kind of safety valve to release the pressure we're under, or times we feel stuck in a situation from which we can't escape on our own. On a personal level, we might use hobbies as a release from a hectic life, or we know that we have family and friends we can rely on for help when we're in a tough spot.

The reality is that when we're feeling pressure, it's important to remember that though it may seem like it, we're never really alone. Just like the defender stuck in the corner with the ball deciding whether to kick it out of bounds or pass to the goalkeeper, we have options and resources available to us; we just have to be willing to use them.

"Start where you are. Use what you have." – Teddy Roosevelt

WATER BREAK: POSSESSION FOR DEVELOPMENT

———————— ⚽ ————————

"Let us say that you and I coach two teams with kids that are 10, 11, and 12 years old and all are about equally good. You try to teach them to play good football, a passing game and with tactical basics while I tell mine to only play long balls and try to shoot. I can assure you that [at first] I will always win against you, by using your mistakes. Break a bad pass and goal. If we however continue with the same training methods during a three year period, you will most likely win every game against us. Your players will have learned how to play while mine haven't. That's how easy it is." – *Laureano Ruiz, FC Barcelona Academy Director*

All the technical and tactical components young players need to learn are built into the possession game. Receiving various types of passes, understanding of space and movement, etc., are all incorporated into a possession style of play. Contrast this with long ball tactics, where (especially in youth soccer), a big strong kid in the back kicks it far to a strong fast kid in attack – thereby bypassing most of the players on the field – teaches kids little aside from kicking the ball with power. Those big fast kids who rely on strength and/or speed generally drop out of the game once their peers catch up physically. Meanwhile, the kids who have been learning a possession game become far superior technically and tactically.

This isn't just a model for teams, but it works for players as well. Think about this from a kid's perspective. If you're playing a sport that features a ball, wouldn't you want to play with it? In a possession-oriented style, the patterns develop naturally where, in effect, everyone shares the prize and has the opportunity to make their own decisions. Each player gets to play with it and feel like they contributed while having fun. Players fall in love with the ball, and as a result, practice with it more and more on their own so that they get better and better. When you're good at something, it's more likely you'll keep doing it as you grow older.

In the long-ball game, we see the exact opposite. The defender or keeper hoofs the ball to the attacking third, where the fast kid runs after it. The midfield – normally the "engine room" for any team – becomes practically non-existent. Because of its direct nature, the players on long-ball teams don't get much of a chance to share the ball. They might as well be signing up for a track team, considering the focus is more on running than soccer.

If your only solution as a defender is to play kickball, you're not going to learn much. The thing is, there's more to learning the game than merely what happens when the ball is at a kid's feet.

When learning possession, kids can be in an environment that makes it easier to recognize situations and find appropriate solutions to problems presented by the game. As games present an ever-changing array of challenges, players begin asking, "What is the game asking of us?"

In many ways learning in soccer is different from other sports. In other sports, training is often done in a "drill" format, where players perform repetitive functions. This isn't optimal for soccer, as by its nature the game is less reliant on plays per se, but rather on the problem-solving ability of players based on certain situations.

There is so much for a player to process on a soccer field that it is impossible for a coach to dictate every single play. It's a player's game, so the kids have to be able to figure things out on their own.

During training sessions, coaches foster the learning process in part by utilizing games that pose problems on the field – situations the players will face during games. Through these games, coaches ask questions, and players then have the opportunity to develop their own solutions to problems and find out what works best *for them.*

An oft-repeated mantra in soccer is that "the game is the best teacher," and this is true – but only if the game in practice is structured appropriately to teach the right lesson. Yes, we want kids to play at practice; after all the best kinds of learning comes from play. However, it's not a great idea for the coach to just roll the ball out at every training session and hope the kids figure it out.

Coaches use games that are tailor-made to teach specific things. The parameters established by the coach (field size, number of players, time constraints, etc.) are all designed to help players learn not only *how* to solve specific, relevant problems, but *why.*

Understanding the reason for something is the first step in turning technique into skill. This is the difference between drills and games. Drills imply lines and repetition without any real context. So, while yes, *technique* is being taught, *skill* is not, as the player does not understand the reason for the technique or the time and place to execute it. *Games,* on the other hand, offer the environment for the repetition needed for technical instruction while also providing the knowledge of how and why the technique is to be used.

As adults, we know that answering "the why" is critical in everything we do in life. In soccer, the ability to answer that question separates the top players from the rest.

For years much of American youth soccer was predicated on identifying young players with physical attributes (the bigger, stronger, faster kids got picked for better teams at younger ages). Because of their early physical maturity, they excelled early on as they often became over-reliant on just speed or size. Eventually, though, other kids would catch up physically, while those super athletic youngsters stopped improving because they never worked on their ball skills.

On the other hand, players with a "soccer brain," or players who innately understood that they had to solve problems in different ways (e.g., something other than kick the ball and run really fast) became better players in the long run because they made a habit of figuring out "the why."

The game of soccer is fluid and constantly changing. Practice should be the same. The only thing a player learns standing in line is how to stand in a line. Humans learn by doing, so let the kids learn the game by playing the game. Given time to play, kids will develop an intuitive understanding of the sport. During these games, kids have the opportunity to experiment and refine their technique, develop their awareness, and hone their decision-making skills. Coaches benefit as it becomes easier to assess and correct these same elements.

The idea is that at the end of the day, the player solves the problem and can then integrate the concept into the larger game.

Training sessions that replicate the chaos of a real game force players to think rapidly on their own. Small-sided games offer players a microcosm of the game itself. They take part of the game and provide instruction in bite-sized pieces. They feature all the components found in a real game, just organized in smaller settings.

If you think about it, this sort of compartmentalization is how we develop children in other areas. Kids begin to learn how to interact with others in settings created by adults. Socialization and education are provided in family and school environments, where kids face situations which help them learn about life. In addition to the content of specific classroom subjects, school environments ideally demonstrate norms of behavior that will remain with kids as they enter adulthood.

In a sense, the overall game of life is introduced to children in smaller, safe environments orchestrated by adults – all designed to allow kids to flourish in their own unique ways. It makes sense that soccer is trained in a similar way.

Kids spend all day in school, sitting in a classroom being instructed by a teacher. They certainly don't come to soccer practice and games to stand in line and be told what to do. They need freedom, freedom to make mistakes and freedom to learn the game at their own pace. Coaches can observe and help young players review their decision-making.

It's important to encourage kids to make decisions – whether wrong or right – and then figure out why they made the decision (because sometimes a player will play the right ball but not know why he did it) and then understand what the potential outcomes of that decision could have been.

This is critical – the player should be able to *explain* why he made that decision. Just like in life, we expect our kids to be able to state *why* they made one decision over another. When I was little, the absolute worst thing I could have said to my father was, "I don't know." I didn't realize it then, but now I understand that "I don't know" is basically an attempt to not take responsibility. It represents a decision to not commit to something – it's essentially a failure to put yourself out there. Looking deeper, it's effectively a statement that says I'm not standing for something, and I lack confidence in myself. This is why learning possession soccer is so important.

For a child, the ball represents a special toy that is responsive to what the child does to it. The ball provides instant feedback and teaches the child how to use it through repetition and fun. In a sense, the child develops a relationship with the ball as he slowly learns how to master it. Ball mastery is so important to young player development because when kids don't learn how to control the ball, their overall ability to play the game is significantly reduced. As a result, these players are more likely to ultimately stop playing because the game just isn't fun anymore.

Understandably then, youth coaches spend a lot of time during training sessions on ball work and playing possession-based games. It's the clear foundation for everything in the game. Players need the basic tools in order to execute the decisions they make. Comfort on the ball allows players to think ahead and understand the implications of their choices.

Approximately 70% of kids quit team sports at age 13.[1] The number one reason cited is that the game is no longer fun. *If you never really learned how to play the game – how to manipulate the ball and make it do what you want* – chances are you won't be having fun when your peers can do much more than you.

---

1. Juliana Miner, "Why 70 percent of kids quit sports by age 13," The Washington Post, June 1, 2016, accessed June 2, 2016,

SECTION TWO: DEFENDING

—————— ⚽ ——————

"In football everything is complicated by the presence of the opposing team." – Sartre, French philosopher and playwright

Chapter 16

CONTAIN (DON'T DIVE IN)

———— ⚽ ————

Assessing a problem in order to solve it

"If I have to make a tackle, then I've already made a mistake." –
Paolo Maldini, Italian defender

Kids (all players really) have a natural inclination when defending 1v1 to rush headlong towards the ball and try to steal it away from an opponent. This aggression isn't a bad thing, as it represents a basic desire to win the ball back. But young players must learn that this doesn't mean running around like a headless chicken or in a frenzy, because running headlong into situations doesn't help.

Watch any youth game, and chances are you'll see a defender run full speed towards an opponent with the ball only to see the dribbler deftly touch the ball to the side while the defender runs past like Wile E. Coyote. The challenge for coaches is to get young players to understand that often the most prudent decision is to "contain" the opponent with the ball, to initially close the space between themselves and the opponent quickly but slow their approach as they draw near to the ball in order to keep the opponent in front of them.

The act of containing a player relates to a defender "jockeying" an opponent, preventing her from dribbling past. Defending players are tempted – really tempted – to "dive in" and poke at the ball with their feet. This stabbing attempt against a skilled player typically fails, allowing the attacking player to dribble past. The thing is, for any defender facing an opponent with the ball, it is so tempting to try to poke that ball free because you are *so sure* you'll be able to get it. That initial stab, though, can be just the opening a skilled dribbler needs.

GAME SCENARIO

While this happens all over the field, let's take a look at one example. The opponent's midfield has played a ball up to a forward, who is matched 1v1 against a defender. If the defender gets beat, the forward is in on goal. Rather than attempt a tackle, the defender should do her best to contain the forward, taking a "side-on" stance, forcing the forward in a certain direction. Which way the defender chooses to force the attacker is dependent on a number of variables, such as: can the defender show the forward to her weak foot; can the defender use the touchline as defensive cover; can the defender show the forward to where the defensive help is likely to arrive first?

The job of this first defender is not necessarily to win the ball, but rather to delay the attack until help arrives. Goals are hard to come by in soccer, and you don't want to give one away cheaply. By "containing" the opponent, a defender is helping her team solve an immediate problem. Players who dive in and miss, on the other hand, often hurt their team.

LIFE OBSERVATION

Everyone at some point faces problems that seem bigger than they can handle. In those situations, it's important not to rush to a decision that may make a situation worse. At the same time, identifying the problem and confronting it early is important. Once it's met and known, the scale of the challenge can be better understood and dealt with.

When facing a complex problem, we rarely have the whole answer right away. But taking the first steps quickly to address it paves the way ultimately for a solution. In other words, it's important to meet it quickly in order to understand the threat; "containing" in soccer is much the same. A defender knows she must close down the opponent with the ball as fast as possible, but then calm down, slow down, and assess the threat, all the while keeping the problem in front of her.

Containing a problem doesn't mean hiding it. It means acknowledging the challenge as soon as it arises while you figure out how to solve it (and recognize that it's ok to get help to respond to it). I think any adult can recognize situations like this. The idea of containing the attacker is not that you ignore the problem, but that you isolate it as you figure out the solution. The assessment of the problem is the key here. You don't want to just throw darts at something before you know what it is. By meeting the problem, staying calm and keeping it in front of you, you can prevent further damage so that you can fix it. The idea behind containment is that you don't overreact and permit the problem to become worse.

You don't want to be like that young defender who just runs full speed at the ball and can't slow herself down as the dribbler eases past her. You don't miss the challenge all together while you're rushing to do "something." Actions without thought are at best not helpful, and at worst, devastating.

If you haven't noticed, this is a consistent theme throughout this book. We want our kids to always have their wits about them. We want to foster that inner calmness that allows them to see the bigger challenges so that they can address them intelligently and with fervor.

They need to learn that everything in life is easier if they can manage to "slow the game down," if they can see things as they are and realize that even if they're up against it (no matter how bad it appears), they do have some control over the results.

"Panic causes tunnel vision. Calm acceptance of danger allows us to more easily assess the situation and see the options." – Simon Sinek, English-American author and speaker

Chapter 17

DON'T FOUL

———— ⚽ ————

Remember the big picture

"Attack and defense is the same thing. You defend well; you attack better." – Pep Guardiola

You hear this often throughout a game. It's a reminder for players that when they're defending, their primary job is to contain the opponent and delay their progress. When stuck trying to keep a skilled player at bay, it's tempting to do anything to win the ball. A defending player desperately wants to tackle the ball away and not get beat. Sometimes, an overly aggressive defender can lose their head and end up fouling the player, resulting in a free kick for the other team (occasionally in a dangerous area).

GAME SCENARIO

Often you hear this when a player with the ball has his back to the defender, shielding the ball and waiting for help to arrive. The defending player's only job here is to prevent the player from turning with the ball, to force the player to pass backwards towards his own goal. You often see this in a defending team's attacking third, when a forward or winger is defending high up the field. I know there are exceptions, but let's just say that many attacking players are not the best defenders, and they may get a little antsy to win the ball back. Rather than containing their opponent and trying to force a mistake, they often commit a foul in frustration while attempting to win the ball. When this happens, an opportunity to get the ball in the attacking third and possibly creating a scoring opportunity is lost.

This is but one example; many teams today use a high press, which means that defending teams put pressure on the opposition when the opponent has the ball deep in their defensive third. Often a goalkeeper will play the ball to a center back or outside back near the touchline, and the defending team will work as a unit to make the field as small as possible. The first defender near the ball will apply immediate pressure, while the players near him take away simple passing lanes. The remainder of the team will condense the playing area, moving closer to the ball to prevent the opponent from completing a pass and breaking the press.

In a high press, the first defender will typically be either a forward or a winger, who forces the player with the ball towards the touchline. When timed well and coordinated effectively, the press forces the player with the ball to face his own touchline and shield the ball. In this situation the player has no place to go. He's trapped.

At this point, you often hear a teammate or coach yell, "NO FOUL," as a reminder to just force the player into a mistake. Again, that first defender's job is simply to contain the opponent, not necessarily to win the ball. His job is to apply enough pressure to force the player into either knocking the ball out of bounds or make a bad pass, which will hopefully result in a turnover. Because the pressure is applied high up the field, winning the ball in that position allows for a better chance to score. If the defending team applies pressure in a coordinated way, when the ball is won, they will have a numbers advantage with the ball going forward.

If the defending player is overzealous and commits a foul (even a "soft" one), the advantage is lost as the opposing team wins a free kick and maintains possession. All the hard physical work done by the team in aggressively pressing high is undone by a mental mistake.

LIFE OBSERVATION

We've all experienced those "rush of the head" moments. You and your teammates exerted a great deal of effort to create a certain opportunity, then one person makes a mistake and the opportunity is gone.

Defending as a team requires coordination and an understanding of other players' roles. When one person deviates from that, everything breaks down, forcing others to adjust. Being part of a group requires individuals to be responsible for themselves and the roles they play, understanding that the rest of the group is counting on them to do that.

In the heat of the moment, sometimes emotions take over and the individual steps out of line. In such situations, it's helpful when we get reminders from friends and colleagues to keep things in check and consider the long-term solution. In this instance in a soccer game, the players dueling may have had a number of confrontations in the game when this situation presented itself. It may be to an extent that the referee has noticed their growing feud, and is watching the situation develop, practically expecting a foul to happen.

In those instances, the coach and teammates in our lives need to remind us of the bigger picture, that it's vital to not lose our heads in that situation because the broader goals are more important than any personal feud or concern we're facing.

Soccer is a low-scoring sport, which is why every goal is important. If an opportunity presents itself to win the ball in an advantageous position, that opportunity can't be squandered by a dumb decision. Life is the same way; it throws a lot of opportunities at us, and we need to be able to capitalize on them by remaining in control and remembering what really matters. We all need people in our lives to say to us, "DON'T FOUL."

"When anger rises, think of the consequences." – Confucius

Chapter 18

LOCK THEM IN

———— ⚽ ————

Taking calculated risks

"The opponent is only as good as you allow them to be." – Unknown

The defending team's goal is to make the field as small as possible. In order to do this a good, organized defense will concentrate most of their entire team near the ball. This effectively closes passing lanes and leaves little space for the opponent to play through.

GAME SCENARIO

When might this prompt be used? Maybe the team is down a goal or needs one to win, so they press high up the field, choke off the passing lanes, and block a cleared ball out of bounds forcing the opponent to make a throw-in deep in its defensive third. The coach or one of the players may urge the team to "lock them in," meaning the team should collapse around the throw-in and hope to win the ball back high up the field.

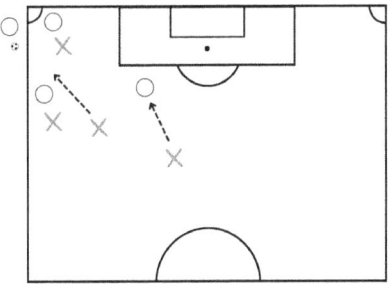

*Defending high against a
throw-in deep in the opponent's
half*

There is some risk to this, as a good long clearance out of the back could lead to a breakaway, so it's not a strategy to use all the time. However, maybe the momentum has switched, and the defending team can feel that energy where they sense a breakthrough is imminent. The moment feels right for a turnover that could lead to an advantage, so now's the time to work together to win the ball back.

LIFE OBSERVATION

If the last chapter recommended caution, this one is more about taking calculated risks. There are moments in life when you feel like maybe the tide could turn if you take a chance and do something aggressive.

For those with a more reticent nature, this can be daunting, but there comes a point when it becomes clear that standing by and watching a situation unfold will not change the outcome. There are certainly times when caution is warranted, that's true. But often, inactivity will not change the outcome, and sometimes, it's necessary to take a risk to prevent an opportunity from being lost.

It's not easy, especially since any risk inherently implies the possibility of losing something you have. In a tied soccer game, a team aggressively pressing the opponent deep in their half late in the game risks exposing themselves defensively. It may mean risking the draw to go for the win. But by being proactive and deciding to apply pressure in a coordinated way, you may force a turnover and get a chance to score.

The inverse, of course, is that doing nothing (effectively being paralyzed by fear and indecision) means that you will lose. Essentially, a leap of faith is needed when it becomes clear that doing nothing (or the same thing you've *been* doing) won't result in the change you're looking for.

Risk is a natural part of life; people take calculated risks all the time. Throughout our lives there are times when some decisions seem riskier than others. You might say they seem like dragons to be faced and overcome (and there are always risks involved in fighting dragons!). In myth, dragons are often found guarding a treasure, and it's up to the hero to overcome the dragon to secure the treasure. "Treasure" is the key word here. Considering the risk is one thing, but with risk comes the reward (the thing we really want). Heroes know, the bigger the treasure, the bigger the dragon.

Imagine a soccer game with only one team on the field. The team can do anything it likes with the ball if there's no opposition. The game is easy. Now add an opposing team who also wants to win. The opponent's goal is to challenge the attacking side, to make it uncomfortable to play against. High pressure involves risk, but no matter how good a team may be, the defending team knows that aggressive pressure poses challenges for anyone.

What we learn as we go through life is that nothing comes for free, and sometimes you must take a chance to get what you want. Learning to be proactive, to stand up for yourself and force a favorable resolution is a big part of life. Just as a defending team takes a risk by aggressively trying to win a turnover, so we must learn to take a chance and try something that might change the outcome for our favor.

"Fairy tales do not tell children dragons exist. Children already know dragons exist. Fairy tales tell children that dragons can be killed." – Neil Gaiman, paraphrasing GK Chesterton

Chapter 19

WIN SOMETHING

———— ⚽ ————

Defining who we become through consistency

"The great victory, which appears so simple today, was the result of a series of small victories that went unnoticed." – Paulo Coelho, Brazilian lyricist and novelist

Pay attention, and you will see there are little battles that happen all over the field. One example relates to shielding the ball near the touchline. There are typically many times during a game where a defender has the ball near the touchline with seemingly nowhere to go. Rather than lose the ball to a pressuring opponent or clearing it out of bounds, he knocks the ball off his opponent and wins a throw-in, thereby keeping possession for his team. In a similar vein, think of a forward holding off a defender near the corner flag. If he can't make a productive pass, can he knock it off the defender and maybe win a corner?

GAME SCENARIO

At some point, a soccer player finds himself in a duel with a particular player throughout the game. Regardless of formations or tactics, the pattern of a game typically finds two opponents facing off against each other throughout a match. The game sometimes lends itself to these battles, and when it does, the players often encounter each other multiple times during the game. As the game goes on, the outcome of these separate battles will leave a psychological "plus" or "minus" with the players. Each event may seem minor in and of itself, but every small victory in these battles will affect the ultimate result of the game, as every positive situation results in a net positive for the team.

As mentioned above, a common situation involves players focused on the ball near the touchline or goal line. A typical battle happens over the ball, as both players try to win possession for their team. It's similar to a 50-50 situation, where both teams are seeking an advantage. Who can win something for their team in that particular moment?

LIFE OBSERVATION

Life is full of struggles. We are constantly struggling, always fighting small battles throughout the day, often with ourselves, sometimes with others. Our attitude and focus in these struggles is important in determining the outcome. If we are fully invested in the present moment, in the particular battle (while understanding its broader implications), the result is more likely to be in our favor.

Note that the immediacy of the moment requires our attention, but it is partly up to the coach to explain why a particular battle matters to the overall effort. We don't want to be thinking that we're wasting our time, thinking that what happens in an instant doesn't matter. Everyone needs to understand that their actions and words matter, and *why* they matter.

This sense of purpose is critical to our development as individuals. It gives us meaning. Players need to understand why they are waging a particular battle on the field, just as we need to understand why we do certain things during the day. During a soccer game, winning a throw-in may not seem significant when taken out of context. However, that same play may leave a positive mental imprint on the player who won the duel and on his teammates.

At the time, the players are probably not considering the larger impact of winning a throw-in, and this is something a coach and teammates can help with. The fact that the player engaged in the battle and won the ball may be indicative of the player's and team's mindset. These little moments and actions illustrate a champion's mentality.

Those little battles each of us fight throughout the day help define who we are, little by little. Our daily actions and habits form the foundation of our character, one brick at a time. Understanding the need to put forth our best effort and following through on that impulse – in every single thing we do – creates habits that enable us to succeed as adults.

Fighting those small battles in the right spirit makes us stronger mentally and emotionally. Regardless of whether or not the moment is won or lost, the willingness to fight and do our best gives us confidence. Small victories (small achievements in what we do) lead to greater victories down the line. Every high school athlete who has run wind sprints has heard a coach scream about not stopping short of the line. It's another reminder to give it your all even in seemingly small things. Don't cheat yourself out of savoring those small victories.

"Excellence is an art won by training and habituation. We do not act rightly because we have virtue or excellence, but we rather have those because we have acted rightly. We are what we repeatedly do. Excellence, then, is not an act but a habit." – Aristotle

Chapter 20

BOUNCING BALL

———— ⚽ ————

Taking notice of things

"Enthusiasm is everything. It must be taut and vibrating like a guitar string." – Pele

S occer, at its best, sees the ball being zipped around the field with crisp passes along the ground. Sometimes, however, the ball pops into the air, either from an aerial pass or a poor touch. Balls on the ground are easier to control, requiring less time for a player to receive and play the next pass. As mentioned before, time and space are everything in soccer. If a pass is easy to control, the player on the ball has more time to decide what to do next, and the defending team must work harder to limit the space to play in. A player trying to control a bouncing ball, however, needs more time to bring the ball down to her feet and execute the next decision, and that provides an opening for defenders to put pressure on the ball.

GAME SCENARIO

This happens all the time at every level of the game. Maybe after a long clearance or a long cross-field switch, a player struggles to control a ball that is bouncing. In youth soccer, a lot of defenders miss this important cue. When a player is trying to settle and control a bouncing ball, the defender must put her opponent under immediate pressure as she has an opportunity to win the ball and begin a counterattack. If a player is allowed to bring the ball down with little pressure, then she maintains the advantage. She can face her defender and has the edge if she decides to take her on 1v1.

Often you may hear a coach yell, "Bouncing Ball!" as a reminder to her players to put her opponent under pressure. A defending team does not want to allow the opponent to be comfortable and control the ball. Controlling the ball makes it easier to control the game. Making the opponent uncomfortable by putting her under pressure and interrupting her rhythm is a key defensive tactic.

If a defender gives an opponent the time to settle the ball, she has lost an opportunity. Learning to identify such moments when opportunity presents itself is so important. The bobble of that bouncing ball offers the defender a brief glimpse of an opportunity. That moment appears as if a door opened just for a moment. Can she be ready to walk through it?

LIFE OBSERVATION

Sometimes in life we hesitate when presented with an opportunity. A bouncing ball resembles an opportunity. It's something that the attacking player doesn't yet have control over and is available if the defender seizes the chance to get it. It's not quite a 50/50 ball, but it offers a window of opportunity that allows a defender the chance to win the ball. There are those moments in life when we see something that isn't really obvious yet presents itself as an opportunity if we're prepared and are willing to react to a situation when we see it.

Like all the cues we've discussed, recognition of these moments requires training and preparation so that when the moment comes, we're ready.

Much of our life revolves around routine. We see the same people, situations, and patterns. We may not notice, but even the most ordinary events in our lives feature unexpected moments. Conversations and encounters – even ones that appear repetitive, may in fact include surprises we are unknowingly numb to. But if we are aware, we'll notice them, and if we notice them, we can respond differently.

As we get mired in our daily routines it's sometimes easy to forget the wonder of the smallest things. The smile from a friend, a hug from Mom...though these events may happen often, we sometimes take them for granted.

This brings up the idea of "ritual vs routine." Think about any ritual which you may have observed or taken part in. For example, sitting in a beautiful church during a wedding ceremony, surrounded by lit candles and beautiful music, conveys a sense of reverence and awe. Or a graduation ceremony, with participants dressed in robes for the occasion, marks out this event from others. Participation in any ritual features individual intention, awareness, and focus. Contrast this with the notion of routine, however, and you realize that the latter implies thoughtlessness and lack of focus or awareness, even to the extent of creating a sort of "blindness," (i.e., you feel as if you could do it in your sleep).

In sporting terms, you could say that a game is a *ritual*. For a player, the game should bring heightened awareness, a focus that enables a player to see the opportunity when an opponent is struggling with a bouncing ball.

If we treat the events of our day as something akin to rituals rather than routines, such an attitude will renew our focus and generate a different energy. Rituals are important because they bring *intention* to what we do. The heightened focus that comes from this attitude enables us to see things differently.

Just to clarify, I'm not talking about tying your shoes. But what if, in the ordinary course of our day, we simply took the time to really think about what we're doing? Rather than go through the motions as people often do, what if we instead renewed our focus to view things intentionally? In these days of social media distractions, a new buzzword is to practice "presence," to take the time to see things as they really are. We might be surprised at what we find (and notice things we've been missing).

In a soccer game, coaches expect defenders to notice and pounce on that bouncing ball. When such moments occur off the field, will you be ready to take advantage? It's not often in life that we receive a written invitation to pursue something. It's important to prepare and stay aware, so that we're ready to go after it when the opportunity presents itself.

"The secret of success in life is for a man to be ready for his opportunity when it comes." – Benjamin Disraeli, Statesman and former Prime Minister of the U.K.

Chapter 21

WHEN ONE GOES, WE ALL GO

— ⚽ —

Taking initiative

"If the enemy leaves a door open, you must rush in." – *Sun Tzu*

When defending, coaches train players to look for basic triggers that should prompt a quick response to certain situations. Sometimes these triggers refer to something the opponent does, and sometimes what our teammates do.

GAME SCENARIO

Let's say the opponent has the ball and is passing it around in its defensive third. We're in good defensive shape and most passing lanes are cut off. At some point our forward has put pressure on an opposing midfielder who turns and passes the ball backwards. Many defensive teams use a backwards pass as a trigger for the entire defensive team to move forward and apply instant pressure.

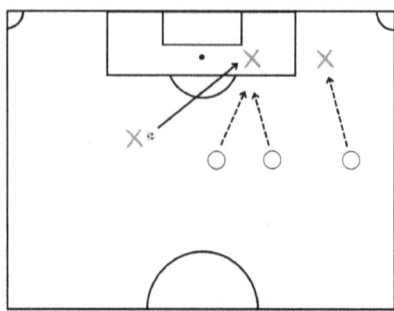

Applying pressure deep in the attacking third

In this case, when the ball is played backwards our forward sprints after it and the intended receiver of the pass. Even if his teammates did not recognize what the backwards pass means, they should recognize the effort of the forward and instantly move to try to make the field as small as possible, hoping to limit the opponent time and space. The goal here is to close off the passing lanes and allow the pressure to force the defender to put his dead down. At that point the ball can either be stolen directly or the player could be forced into kicking the ball long or out of bounds, which (either way) should allow our team to regain possession.

The point is for the team to recognize the "one" who is applying pressure and then make sure the entire team reacts together as a unit. While most players can handle individual pressure either by themselves or with the help of teammates, a concerted press cuts off all avenues of escape. You could make the analogy of a scene in a battle – instead of making one soldier go it alone, the entire unit works together to overrun the enemy.

In a sense it becomes a sort of battle cry, "When one goes, we all go." This might not be one that is heard often, but it's a message I have shared with my teams.

LIFE OBSERVATION

Understanding the common mission within a group (and the individual understanding of particular roles) offers people the freedom to make their own decisions in the spur of a moment if they think an action will help. In this case, when one player recognizes the trigger to go, his teammates see it as well and react accordingly.

In training, part of the reason coaches teach the principles of play through small-sided games is so that players (regardless of position) can recognize triggers on their own and take the appropriate action according to the situation. In a soccer game, roles change continuously not because of assigned positions, but due to players' proximity to teammates, opponents, the ball, and other factors. Part of the beauty of soccer is that depending on the situation, every player is alternately a quarterback, or a linebacker, or a wide receiver. The ability to think and act on the fly with the support of teammates is paramount.

Training players to seize the initiative and take action based on what they see also means we're training them in leadership, because leaders are not afraid to take initiative when they need to. Coaches showing players that they trust them to make their own decisions on the field inspires confidence and is a critical component of developing not just the player, but the whole person.

Most of our lives are spent in groups. Working with others, we learn there are times to lead as well as follow. The roles we play often change, and it's important to remember that it's the group's mission that matters, rather than specific roles.

We learn how important it is to support each other as we combine our efforts on behalf of a common goal. "When one goes, we all go" calls for cohesive movement of the entire team. In this scenario, the forward is the "one," and if the rest of the team doesn't recognize the press is happening, then the forward is likely wasting his energy, as the opponent will find it easy to pass around a lone defender. If the team goes together, however, the group will have a better chance of success.

During the invasion of Normandy on D-Day in World War II, it has been widely recognized that non-commissioned and junior officers (rather than field commanders) took it upon themselves to make quick decisions that enabled the Allies to win the day. Under the stress of battle and chaos, the chain of command was significantly disrupted. If not for the bravery and initiative of young soldiers caught in the thick of the action, the outcome could have been much different.

Of course, most of us don't spend our days facing life-and-death decisions, but we do spend much of our lives as members of organizations (e.g., school, work, religious affiliation, etc.). While participating in these groups, we also assume their goals. It is necessary, therefore, to understand our roles within those organizations, and how the role we play affects certain outcomes.

This understanding of a group's core mission is essential for individuals in order to frame their decision-making. We want to teach kids that when part of an organization, it's important to understand what it is the group is trying to achieve. They can then train themselves so that they can recognize situations and have the confidence to take necessary action.

Knowing what the overall objective is enables individuals to think through problems, act, and provide reasoning for their decisions. This is what we want to instill in young people. We don't want them to become robots, we want them to grow into individuals who are willing to take initiative within organizations and support others who do the same.

"Nothing is more difficult, and therefore more precious, than to be able to decide." – Napoleon Bonaparte

Chapter 22

MARK UP

⚽

Embracing responsibility

"Soccer is simple. You just need to have the right mentality, fighting in every game, in every practice, and for every ball." – Hristo Stoichkov, former Bulgarian forward and 1994 Ballon d'Or winner

Anyone who has ever watched a soccer game has heard this; on almost every defending set piece, the goalkeeper and/or coach screams this at her players. Whether it's a corner or free kick, the message is for the players to find an opponent and cover her on the play (I acknowledge that tactically, there has been a movement towards zonal defending in these situations, but that's an argument for another day).

GAME SCENARIO

Players often call out their "mark" to teammates (e.g., "I've got 9!"), letting them know who they are covering on the play. Their "mark" becomes their responsibility as the game becomes a number of 1v1 battles, with defenders doing what they can to prevent their opponent from scoring. To the greatest extent possible, the defending team seeks to match up with opponents of similar size and athletic ability. This is why you may often see a tall center forward marking a tall central defender from the other team, even though you may not think of a forward as a "defender" in the typical sense.

These situations are ideal comparisons for life. In the fluidity of a game, players can argue that a mistake wasn't really their fault. In these dead ball situations, however, players are forced to accept *individual responsibility* for their actions, because in this setup, everyone knows whose mark got free. They know (and often so does everyone else in the game) who bore responsibility.

An extra factor here is that every team has one or two players whom everyone on the field knows are the "targets" for the set piece. Given that the ball that is served will likely be in the air, there are normally a couple of specialists who are adept at scoring headers. They will have an advantage because set pieces in soccer are practiced, and the attacking team will know where the ball is going. This makes it more difficult for the individual defenders accepting the responsibility for marking these targets, as they know that they will face the challenging prospect of taking on the opponent's "best" players in this situation.

LIFE OBSERVATION

Yes, soccer is a team sport. But within every team, individual responsibility still remains. Without individuals holding themselves and each other accountable, the team will fail.

Successful players thrive in an environment where high standards are the expectation, and individual accountability is the norm. Each player has a job to do and is expected to do that job to the best of her ability. This is not to say that mistakes and failures happen; of course they do, all the time. But the willingness to accept responsibility for one's actions is paramount.

Even if we're part of a group, as individuals, we often find ourselves in situations where we're on our own but with a particular task that is important for the group. It may feel as if we're isolated on an island, or that we're underneath a spotlight highlighting what we're doing, all with an opponent actively trying to beat us.

The thing is, we want to cultivate that desire to take on responsibility in children so that when they grow up, they'll be comfortable with it. Being accountable carries with it a bit of pressure but facing it during a youth soccer game is a relatively safe precursor to what kids will face as they get older.

A sense of individual responsibility should begin early; from expectations of picking up toys as a toddler to following through on commitments as kids get older, it's a critical part of life. Think about adults you know. Those who are responsible and who hold themselves accountable for their actions are held in high regard and are often the ones who are asked (and are willing) to take on challenging tasks.

Embracing responsibility is the foundation for forging independence and leadership. Willingness to be held accountable, to undertake challenges (and accept that things may go wrong) is the underpinning of leadership.

We all want our children to do more than the bare minimum. We want them to excel and become the best version of themselves.

To do this, they need to be comfortable with accountability. Being responsible for one's deeds demonstrates honesty, which is a clear sign that they can be trusted, and we all want people in our lives who we know can be trusted.

A willingness to be accountable in small things such as man-marking in a youth soccer game is good practice for being responsible for more important matters as adults. The successes and failures that kids experience on a soccer field will help prepare them for their future.

"The price of greatness is responsibility." – Winston Churchill

Chapter 23

HOLD THE 18

⚽

Enough is enough

"Your number 1 priority as a defender is to keep the ball out of the back of the net." – Kelley O'Hara, two-time World Cup winner

A s mentioned previously, defending is all about managing space. This is particularly clear on set pieces.

Defenders on the 18-yard line defending a free kick

GAME SCENARIO

Let's say there is a free kick that's too far away for a realistic shot, so the ball will likely be played into the penalty area for someone to receive it and try to score. The attacking team will want to use as much space as they possibly can, stretching the field as high as possible. The defending team, on the other hand, wants to do the opposite, using the offside rule to limit the space behind and effectively "shorten" the field by forming a line well away from their own goal. The default here is typically the top of the penalty area, or "the 18."

Once the foul is called, and the attacking team is preparing to take its free kick, either the goalkeeper or the central defender will usually begin organizing the defense, ultimately yelling, "HOLD THE 18!" At this point the defenders will form a line parallel to the stripe at the top of the penalty area. Attacking players will begin jockeying for position on this line while defenders will "mark up" an opposing player. Because of the offside rule, the attackers can't get behind the defensive line until the ball is kicked, so the defenders are required to remain vigilant, holding their line while trying to prevent their opponent from beating them in a footrace towards goal.

LIFE OBSERVATION

The battlefield cry to "HOLD THE LINE" is in almost every war movie ever made. In a sense, this is what the defensive team is trying to do. It's a situation where an individual or group has some advantage over you, yet you do have *some* level of control. In this case you can shape the environment to limit the edge they have. A simple example is how a smaller military force, when facing a larger enemy, chooses where and when to fight a battle using terrain to give them an advantage. In sport, we're always trying to limit the advantages of our opponents. If we know our opponent is left-footed, we try to force them to their right. If there is a size mismatch, we look to exploit it. We do this all the time in life as well.

But what about those times when we're limited in what we can do? When we feel stuck and can't seem to find a way out of a tough spot? It sometimes feels as if all we can do is "limit the damage," as if we're pinned back by something. Sometimes the best we can do is "hold the line," to do whatever we can to give ourselves a chance. It's not ideal, but maybe the best we can do in those moments is draw the line and say, "Enough is enough." Things may have been bad, but now I have found a place where I *can* exert some control over a situation.

Think of an introverted student who must make a presentation to his class. In the days leading up to the presentation, he's petrified, incredibly frightened to speak in public (especially to his peers). As he prepares his talk, he will do whatever he can to make that experience go well. In addition to rehearsing his talk over and over again, maybe he finds funny props or visual aids, or some audio background, or he dresses up in a special outfit, all geared to get his classmates to laugh and be interested. He'll do anything he can to change the environment to give himself a better chance of success.

We're constantly seeking ways – especially in situations when we're challenged and feel like we're behind the 8-ball – to give ourselves some kind of advantage to level the playing field and give ourselves a chance. Every one of us is moving forward through life. As we grow and mature, we find that life sometimes feels like an endless series of trials. When we're tested, we need to find ways to respond to the challenge, particularly when we seem to be backed into a corner. Finding ways out of those corners and move on to the next challenge is a big part of life – and one that helps us to grow into who we were made to be.

"Tough times never last, but tough people do." – Robert H. Schuller, motivational speaker

Chapter 24

AWAY - BE SAFE - CLEAR IT

The wisdom of prudential decisions

"Possession means nothing when the opponent takes its chances."
— Franz Beckenbauer, World Cup winner as player and coach

These are a little different from each other, but the meaning is essentially the same. You'll hear this call either from defenders or a coach, instructing a player near her own goal to get the ball out of danger, to either kick it far up the field or just knock it out of bounds, as pressure is coming fast and you don't want to lose the ball in a dangerous part of the field.

GAME SCENARIO

You'll often hear a goalkeeper yell, "AWAY!" to a defender who is in her own penalty area, typically during some kind of goalmouth scramble. Basically, in order to prevent a goal, it means, *just get the ball out of there.* "CLEAR IT" is essentially the same thing. "BE SAFE" is a little different; it tells a defender to just play it out of bounds; don't try something fancy as there is pressure you don't know about. It also gives the defender (who is trying to figure out what to do) an easy solution to a problem.

This is typically called when the defensive player is likely to get to the ball before an attacker, but she has limited options. Whether she's caught with the ball near the touchline, or in her own penalty area defending a corner, the defender's job is to get the ball out of danger. When a defender hears this, she knows to put the ball high and wide in order to give the defending team some breathing room.

LIFE OBSERVATION

Sometimes in life, whether at work, or school, or in relationships, there does come a time where we have to simply "play it safe," no matter how bold we wish to be. It might be a business deal that someone wants to close but knows that pushing the issue may mean forcing her potential client's business elsewhere. An even simpler example might be when an inexperienced skier recognizes that the double black diamond mogul run might not be the best option that day.

The point is not that a player should never try something, rather in that particular situation it is better to play safe in order to take hold of the opportunity at a better time. We spoke of awareness earlier; it is important to know your environment and recognize what the moment is asking. Sometimes less is more; sometimes it's best to take a step back and live to fight another day.

You're probably reading this and thinking, "Wait a minute... this whole book is about *not* doing this." And you're right; but as the saying goes, sometimes discretion is the better part of valor. I mean, despite what you see in the movies, you don't try to fight a mugger with a gun. You don't go swimming during a lightning storm.

The point is, there are times when, yes, it's OK to "play it safe." Life isn't about absolutes; sometimes we find ourselves in situations that aren't ideal, and we have to "make do" as best as we can. Often in these situations a little caution is warranted to make sure it doesn't get worse! To borrow from American football, you don't typically go for it on 4th down; usually you punt.

Back to soccer, maybe at this point in the game the defense has been under tremendous pressure and is exhausted. It's clear that they need a moment to recharge and get organized. Clearing the ball away offers the defenders a moment to catch their breath and figure out some solutions. That's what we're really talking about here.

Awareness breeds prudential decision-making. Sometimes, when things are not going your way, rather than forcing something, it may be best to remember that the game doesn't end on one play. There are *always* more plays to make.

One of the things I love about soccer is that every player is a two-way player. One moment you might be tracking down the opposing forward and the next you're dribbling by two opponents and serving up a perfect cross.

This should offer some perspective. Regardless of age, people naturally tend to get caught up in the immediate needs of the moment. A little perspective is healthy, offering us a reminder that, simply, tomorrow is another day. While we may at times feel like we're stuck in a rut we can't seem to get out of, it's helpful to remember that those moments don't define us.

As difficult as it can be to believe sometimes, we will have opportunities to respond anew, and if we must temporarily do something to "take a breather," then that's OK.

What befalls us isn't important; how we respond is.

"Great ability without discretion comes almost invariably to a tragic end." – Leon Gambetta, French statesman

WATER BREAK: TOTAL FOOTBALL

———— ⚽ ————

Soccer is known as the Simple Game; there are only 17 laws of the game. About half of these are just guidelines regarding field dimensions, markings, and the ball. The latitude that such generality provides truly invites a creative imagination. The game is fluid; tactical schemes and the possibilities for individual inventiveness are wide open. Soccer is *the* democratic game, offering players almost unrestricted freedom to play the game as they see fit.

This freedom that exists for soccer players is unique; no other team sport makes allowances for (indeed encourages) the individual to demonstrate his creativity within the team environment. Defenders can score at any time; there are no timeouts; no player is limited to a particular section of the field but rather is allowed the independence to use his own intellect and ability to make his mark on the game.

This is all great for kids as children need and crave the freedom to discover how to solve problems.

In soccer, young players need to learn how to both attack and defend and figure out solutions based not on specific positional roles, but rather on where they are on the field vis-à-vis their teammates and opponents.

Nowhere is this more evident than in a system of play called, "Total Football."

Total Football...among other things, an idea that every player can play any position on the field. In this concept, every player understands not only his own specific positional roles and responsibilities but maintains a broader understanding of game principles so that he understands what should be done in different parts of the field in different situations.

The basic idea behind Total Football is that any outfield player can interchange positions with any other. It's intended to be an inherently fluid system in which freedom of movement and individual creativity is encouraged, all while maintaining its organizational structure.

Now it is perfectly normal in any system of play that from time-to-time teammates will interchange positions with other players. Under the concept of Total Football, however, this interchange is taken to another level, whereby the Left Wing might somehow be found playing Right Back!

When in possession, players are free to move around to provide numerical advantages where necessary. Players make these decisions not based on their prescribed positions, but rather on the principles of the game. This requires intelligent players who can read the game well, and who have the versatility, the understanding, and the bravery to take the initiative and responsibility to *immediately* step into another role in the system as the situation demands. The system requires that players be willing to step out of their comfort zones on a regular basis.

As Peter Parker's Uncle Ben in the Spiderman comics said, "With great power comes great responsibility." If the old maxim "knowledge is power" is true, then as players develop and learn more about the tactical elements of the game they should be encouraged to look beyond their own specific duties. In order to develop individual responsibility, young players need to be challenged to step into a role (even if it is unnatural for them) for the sake of the team.

There is an old adage in sports that, "Good players make *themselves* better. Great players make *their team* better." Great players know that it's not enough to focus solely on themselves. The best players are always asking themselves how they can help the team, not just when they have the ball, but all game long. Elite teams are filled with players like this, individuals who prioritize the team over themselves. *That mindset* spread throughout the group is what makes a team pretty special.

This is where understanding game principles is vital. It doesn't matter what your position is; what's important is your willingness to answer that question (*what is the game asking* of you at that moment). Contrast this idea with what happens all too often in youth soccer...when young players are limited by coach to certain roles in certain areas of the field. When that happens, those players – and their teams – will suffer and be at a disadvantage.

You could say that Total Football constitutes a more enhanced team scenario, in that each player understands and can recognize the given needs of his team and how he should move with or without the ball. The player recognizes the impact of his decision and acts according to the team's needs at that moment. The fact that he must leave his initial positional placement is irrelevant, as he knows the team's goals are the primary concern, and that he has the trust that his teammates will fill his original space on the field of play after he moves into someone else's.

This is essentially the ethic of putting the team's goals ahead of the individual. The act of doing more than what is asked of you for the group's benefit. Contrast this with the staid, somewhat standard models of youth coaching ("You're a defender; don't cross midfield!"), which at best is a limiting proposition. At worst, the rigid positioning system inherent in much of youth soccer inhibits a player's technical development and worse, actually limits freedom and offers a refuge from responsibility. This is the direct opposite of what we should be encouraging. Coaches need to challenge young players to step out of their comfort zone, purposefully putting players in situations that will help them learn something new.

So why on Saturday mornings do you see young "defenders" run up to the midfield line and stop as if they're afraid of entering a forbidden zone (the attacking half)? I sometimes think that a rigid focus on positions may be the biggest single impediment to the development of young players. "Johnny, you're a right defender; under no circumstance do you cross midfield. And stay on the right side!!"

What if Johnny had the ball and wanted to dribble forward? He won't because he'll take his instructions literally. Instead, he'll simply get to the midfield line and kick the ball, probably to the other team. But what if Johnny were allowed some freedom to be creative and make his own decisions? I highly doubt that Antonee Robinson's youth coach told him to stay in his own half.

In today's world, we sometimes misunderstand what freedom really is. Many think that freedom simply means the right to do what we want, but as Saint John Paul II said, "Freedom consists not in doing what we like, but in having the right to do what we ought."

The freedom inherent in soccer (particularly under Total Football) is an advantage only if the individual players recognize situations and take the responsibility to act in the best interests of the team. Just as a jazz musician plays his part in harmony with his bandmates so that his solo is part of a coherent piece, so must soccer players work together to creatively make the whole greater than the sum of individual parts.

In life, we are not really burdened by many legal mandates dictating how we are to live. Few laws regulating our lives means that we are free to express ourselves in myriad ways. Humans are made to create, and we have the freedom to do so. Likewise, the minimal number of laws governing the game of soccer provides the perfect environment for individual freedom and creativity to flourish in a team setting.

The beauty of the game allows players to recognize that freedom but also to couple it with responsibility. The best coaches understand that all players need some freedom to make their own decisions. More importantly, fostering understanding about the responsibility that comes with freedom is a critical lesson to learn for any young person.

SECTION THREE: TRANSITION

——————— ⚽ ———————

"The chief aim of order is to give room for good things to run wild." – GK Chesterton

Chapter 25

FIRST MAN

———— ⚽ ————

The importance of responding to a mistake

"I want my players chasing the ball like (dogs chase) dog bones." –
Pep Guardiola

When defending, "first man" refers to the first defender, or the defender closest to the ball. As seen before, that player's job is to apply pressure to the opponent with the ball. His decision-making, movement, and body position dictate what the rest of the defensive team does.

When the ball is given away, the easiest time to win the ball back is immediately after it is lost. The player who lost the ball is typically the one who needs to put immediate pressure on the ball winner, whose head is likely down, looking at the ball after a tackle. It's important to emphasize that it doesn't matter what this player's position is; once he loses the ball, he is a defender. It's his job to pressure the ball carrier right away, as his teammates will react to his movements. Pressure is applied as a group, as the individuals seek to take up positions that will block every passing lane based on the shape of the first defender, preventing the opposition from getting forward quickly.

Without this pressure, the other team has a chance to keep the ball and develop their own attack on goal. When a team wins the ball, they often have the opportunity to attack quickly. Consequently, immediate pressure is important to prevent a quick counterattack.

GAME SCENARIO

Let's look at this example. A midfielder has just lost the ball near the touchline. The opponent who just won the ball has his head down focused on trying to control the ball and is figuring out what to do next. This is the easiest time to win the ball back. As soon as the player who lost the ball gets to work pressuring the opponent, there is an opportunity to win the ball back quickly, whether from a mis-control or an errant pass because of pressure.

The rest of the team responds to the pressure and the players work to take away the simple passing lanes. The best illustration of this may have been the FC Barcelona teams under Pep Guardiola. Those teams, given their outstanding technical ability, played a short passing game, allowing them to always have numbers around the ball. When they did lose it, they had the "six second rule," which meant that when anyone lost the ball, the entire team would go into an aggressive press for six seconds to try to win the ball back. More often than not it worked; because they were so close together, they were able to apply pressure as a cohesive unit, forcing the opponent's head down while taking away the passing lanes. Only after six seconds would they fall back and defend until another trigger to press happened.

LIFE OBSERVATION

Let's be honest; nobody likes making a mistake (even though it happens all the time). I mentioned this earlier; as we grow older, one of the most important lessons we must learn is that so often it's not the mistake that matters, but rather our response to the mistake. Everyone makes mistakes; nobody's perfect. These are all things we know but sometimes we don't accept them when it comes to our own shortcomings. Our first reaction to a mistake might be to drop our heads and be self-critical, but that is not what we are called to do. Our first instinct must be to move forward and react in the best possible way. What is happening now? Yes, the mistake happened, but what can we do right now, at this moment to rectify that mistake?

Once something bad happens there is nothing we can do except control our reaction. We must train ourselves to prepare for mistakes, to expect them so that we can react instantaneously, without hesitation. Nobody is perfect, and we know in sport that there is no such thing as a perfect game.

During a soccer game, the ball is lost countless times. It's a fact. Coaches want players who are brave and who play with personality, willing to take on one or more defenders. When players do this, they're bound to make mistakes and lose the ball. There are two points to consider here. We want to make sure that over the course of a game the player has the confidence to try again, but we also expect him to help the team in that moment. As soon as he loses the ball his teammates count on him to react and work hard to win the ball back.

Most teams have one or two of those players who are skillful and love to dribble (and sure, they may occasionally act like prima donnas). When they're on the ball they may seem to be playing for themselves, but as soon as they lose it, they need to learn how important it is to defend immediately and work hard for the team.

No matter who we are, our mistakes followed by our personal reactions to those mistakes are what ultimately turn us into the people we are. Just like in a soccer game, we all make countless mistakes at work and in relationships. How we respond to those mistakes determines who we will be. Do we act selfishly and sulk? Do we blame others? Or do we regroup and figure out a way forward as quickly as possible?

The timing of the reaction is important. We face setbacks all the time, yet when we have the wherewithal to respond immediately, we can often mitigate the negative consequences. In soccer we may lose the ball but if we react quickly enough, we may prevent the other team from scoring a goal. In all aspects of our lives sometimes things don't go the way we expect them to, but it's important to remember that our story doesn't end; there's always a job to do.

It might be the need for the admission of a wrong, or an unpleasant conversation, or a temporary fix to a long-term solution. Either way, the quicker we respond to the mistake, the better. As an example, after getting a bad grade on a test, rather than pouting and complaining, a student would be better served by recognizing what went wrong and seeking help (whether from a teacher or fellow student) to make sure that he doesn't make the same mistakes.

Few things in life really go according to plan. Simply understanding this, and preparing accordingly, enables us to ride the challenges life throws at us and make sure we continue to move forward.

"The best laid plans of mice and men often go awry." – Robert Burns

Chapter 26

GET BEHIND THE BALL

———— ⚽ ————

The importance of quick reactions

"What's the most important play in soccer? The next one." – Bora Milutinovic, U.S. Coach in 1994 World Cup

O nce the ball is lost, the first instinct players should have is to get "behind the ball," which simply means that all players should drop back and get between the ball and their own goal.

You might hear this when the ball is lost in the attacking third or in midfield. All players need to remember that regardless of their position, everyone is a defender when their team doesn't have the ball. As we've discussed, a basic team defensive tactic is to get everyone behind the ball and limit the space that a team has to play forward.

GAME SCENARIO

Let's say the ball is lost by a right winger in the attacking third while the forward, left winger, and attacking midfielder were all making runs toward goal, anticipating the cross. All too often these players put their heads down in frustration. They had been anticipating a big play, but were thwarted. You may then hear teammates or coaches direct the players to "get behind the ball." It's a significant cue for those players to wake up because they are needed in the next phase of play. While one player puts pressure on the ball, the other players know they need to drop back and take away passing lanes to limit the opponent's attacking options.

The team that wins the ball will naturally try to break forward quickly. If you can make them pause their attack, you've given yourself a chance. Forcing the opponent to slow down and be more methodical while you regroup is essential. By responding quickly and instantly moving into a good defensive position, a defending team can nullify the opponent's attacking opportunities.

LIFE OBSERVATION

In our game scenario, the attacking team felt good about their play. They were moving towards goal looking for an opportunity to score. Then the tables turned, and they were forced to play defense. We've all had those moments in life where everything seemed to be going so well, when suddenly the roof caves in.

Whether it be school, work, or relationships, there seem to be times when it feels like nothing can go wrong, and then... well, something goes wrong. Maybe you received shocking news; you didn't get the grade you expected, you failed a driver's test, or you didn't get into the college you wanted. Sometimes life throws a monkey wrench into our plans – often in the most unexpected ways.

Whatever it is, the bottom line is that something's gone awry, something must be done to address it, and the quicker you do it the better. As adults, we know that life throws up obstacles all the time. You learn to ride those bumps in the road and continue on. In this instance, a player lost the ball; it happens. If the team responds appropriately, the problem can be solved.

The important thing to remember is that reacting *quickly* to delay the challenge's threat is the first step. What small things can you do to stem the tide so you can figure out how to solve the problem? It's usually something obvious. In this game situation, players react and move quickly to get behind the ball as a first step to defend.

Doing even the smallest thing and taking the simplest action not only gives us time to assess the situation but also just the act of doing something (anything!) gives us confidence and helps to give us some degree of control. We experience failure all the time; the important thing is to recognize when it happens and tackle it right away so you can figure out how to be better and avoid making the same mistakes.

Even in our closest relationships, during a conversation or some other type of encounter, someone may misunderstand our intentions, taking something we said the wrong way, and seemingly out of the blue they respond aggressively. How can you react quickly to defuse the situation so that you can take a step back and figure out what happened before the misunderstanding gets worse?

Doing nothing can have tragic consequences. Not responding in some way can often cause the situation to spiral, making what was a minor problem much worse. Even more damaging, not acting quickly (even while we're trying to figure out the problem) can give off the impression that we don't care enough to respond.

Look, sometimes people freeze in social situations. It may be due to fear, or perhaps they simply aren't sure what the best response should be. It's understandable, but it's important to realize that this inaction can have drastic consequences. Even among friends and family members, we all know that uncorrected misunderstandings can have repercussions that last years. We all make mistakes. That's why it's so important to learn that the best thing we can do is not dwell on them (or really anything from the past) but to act as quickly as possible to prevent the situation from getting worse.

It may seem easy to ignore it or blame someone else. These may be visceral reactions, but it's important to remember that these are your worst options and shouldn't enter your mind. They achieve nothing and only hurt you in the long run. Accept it, address it, and move on. In soccer, reacting quickly and getting behind the ball is a simple action that tells your teammates that you're still engaged and committed to solving the problem.

It's necessary to overcome the initial disappointment, pick your head up, and act. The fluidity of soccer makes for a great life analogy. Just as the play on a soccer field doesn't stop, neither does life. We don't get timeouts. Players learn that it doesn't matter who made the mistake. The group must work together to fix it.

Cultivating a problem-solving mindset (and a willingness to address problems) is an invaluable gift for the young people in our lives. It's easy to get frustrated at times. But just as soccer players learn to react quickly to a turnover, young people need to learn how important it is to respond when life throws a monkey wrench in our plans.

"The appeal of the wild for me is its unpredictability. You have to develop an awareness, react fast, be resourceful and come up with a plan and act on it." – Bear Grylls, British adventurer and writer

Chapter 27

50-50

———— ⚽ ————

Committing to challenges

"You have to fight to reach your dream. You have to sacrifice and work hard for it." – Lionel Messi

E specially at the youth levels, games can often devolve into a series of 1v1 battles, which makes for an ugly game of soccer. Instead of long periods of possession, where players pass and move in intricate patterns, all too often we see a game with a lot of "loose" balls and 50-50 challenges. It's not really what the game should look like, but it happens a lot when coaches do not place a priority on keeping the ball.

Simply, a 50-50 ball means that there is an equal chance that players from opposing teams can reach and gain control of a loose ball. The reality is that there is rarely a perfect "50-50" ball, as it is likely closer to one player than the other. The focus, however, is on the battle to win the ball, and the coach's call, "50-50!" directs players from both teams to charge at the ball at full speed to get there first.

GAME SCENARIO

A 50-50 ball may happen anywhere but is usually seen in midfield. Often a player will have a bad touch and the ball will get away from him, resulting in a loose ball that must be contested. In a perfect world, there would be no 50-50 balls (it goes without saying that we obviously don't live in a perfect world). However, when the ball is lost, it must be won again. In a 50-50 challenge, with both players typically charging as hard as they can to get to the ball first, it requires a bit of courage to essentially not think about the body and try to win the ball.

Much like challenges in life, the 50-50 ball itself can come about in a number of different ways. The cause is irrelevant. Whether from a hard tackle, a goal kick, or an errant pass, etc., the only thing that matters is that it is a loose ball to be won, and the team that wins it gains an advantage. There is a new opportunity, and like most opportunities, courage and a willingness to compete are required to secure it.

LIFE OBSERVATION

Sometimes things in life get away from us, and it takes a bit of bravery to win them back. Those situations demand 100% intention and effort to succeed, no matter the obstacles. Going hard after a 50-50 ball requires a willingness to face a challenge, and that is what life requires of us as well. Remember, the ball represents something a player cherishes. In life we often find ourselves fighting for something we love. It's a reminder that life rarely goes according to plan, and when it falls apart, we have to be willing to muster up the courage to get back on track.

As I mentioned earlier, the reality is there are rarely any true "50-50" balls; most loose balls are going to be easier to secure for one team more than another. However, something close to a 50-50 ball is like life giving a player a second chance to get that thing he really wants. Mistakes happen, challenges present themselves, failure hits us hard. But life goes on. We will get more opportunities. How willing are we to seize that second chance when it comes around? Are we prepared to fight for it? By engaging in a 50-50 challenge a player is telling his teammates that he values them and will fight for them. Like any challenge, to enter into a 50-50 duel requires nerve, determination, commitment, and bravery.

Players are taught to go hard into the challenge in order to win the ball. This is a key point; players who enter the challenge timidly are not only less likely to win the ball but are more prone to injury. Failure to commit 100% when going into a challenge typically results in failure (and possibly some bruises as well!).

Off the field, fully committing oneself to a challenge demonstrates that you care about the problem and are personally invested in finding a solution. You don't have to get everything right; you just need to commit 100% to it, even if it's outside your comfort zone. Learning to fully commit to challenges is so important for personal development. It shows that you care about something. In a game, charging headlong into a 50-50 challenge is illustrative. Such challenges are hard, and your teammates see that by your actions you care about them and about the result of the game.

Apathy is a menace that lurks in all of us, and I think it's fair to say it can be a big problem for kids as well. Learning the value of people and things is a lesson all kids need to understand, even more so in modern society. I've said it before, but one thing that kids deal with today that previous generations never contemplated was social media. "Doomscrolling" can have a numbing effect that leads to an apathetic worldview. Finding things to care about allows a child to invest in something worthwhile. This is critical, because when people say they love something, they place a value on it, and you cannot be apathetic about something you value.

When kids direct their energy into positive activities, they grow and become more responsible. Through small actions (and occasionally big ones), young people may come to understand what is required of them as they mature into adulthood, forge relationships, and invest themselves in important activities, whether it be related to family, work, school, or their community.

The way a young player throws himself into a 50-50 challenge should transfer to other areas. Many kids aren't crazy about school, for example, but school is important and requires commitment.

Life can be hard at times, throwing up obstacles that seem insurmountable. Yet like Sisyphus, we need to keep pushing that boulder uphill. Yes, the result is important, but the effort is the vital thing. People lose all the time, but the effort is what makes people champions.

Giving your best and fighting for what's important stays with you. We don't always get the outcomes we hoped for, but if we gave it our best then we can still hold our heads high. Conversely, failing because we didn't fully commit can lead to regret, which is a haunting feeling.

The beauty of the 50-50 challenge is that talent and skill are secondary to effort. When we put forth the effort for something like a 50-50 ball, we are highlighting the fact that we believe the game has value. We may still fail at the attempt, but by simply committing ourselves totally into the challenge, we demonstrate our commitment to our teammates, the game, and to ourselves.

Investing our time and effort into the people and things we care about gives our lives a purpose beyond ourselves, and that is priceless.

"You cannot love a thing without wanting to fight for it." – GK Chesterton

Chapter 28

SECOND BALL

Seeing the bigger picture and understanding your role

"Life is 10% what happens to you and 90% how you react to it." –
Charles R. Swindoll, Christian pastor

This is one you hear incessantly at games. For some coaches it becomes an irrepressible instinct to yell "SECOND BALL!" at the top of their lungs every time a keeper punts the ball, or a goal kick is launched to midfield. The idea is that two players will fight to win the ball in the air, but because of the action neither will be able to actually hold onto the ball. This first battle for the ball leads to a second loose ball players will have to fight for in order to seek possession.

In the modern game most teams seek to play the ball on the ground out of the back. It ensures that possession will be kept, at least in the short term. A long goal kick or punt from the keeper ends up being (in most cases, anyway) a 50-50 ball (Side note: The number of long balls with 50-50 challenges is typically related to the quality of the game. The higher the number of long balls, the poorer the quality of play. A game with fewer long balls is an indicator that teams are trying to play). Long balls like these used to dominate the game. Today you'll hear parents want to see the goalkeeper play it long because in their mind it means that if the ball is farther away from their own goal, then there is little danger of conceding a goal. In this way of thinking, possession is essentially irrelevant.

GAME SCENARIO

This happens often during most games; a long ball is sent to midfield where two players go up to win a header. When normally in possession, teams spread out in an effort to create more space, making the field "as big" as possible. During these long ball situations, however, players gravitate towards each other, making one area of the field very congested. The reason players do this is to support each other (specifically their teammate who contests for the aerial ball) in an effort to anticipate where the ball will bounce. The first ball is the long ball, and the "second ball" is the loose ball that comes from the players fighting to win the header.

The team that reacts quickest can win the second ball, gain possession, and begin a new attack. From a moment of chaos, order can be restored by the team that wins that second ball. When played well, soccer is normally about coherence (e.g., patterns of play, spacing, intricate passing combinations, organized defensive shape, etc.). Those direct long balls represent an interruption in that pattern. In a sense, anticipating and winning the second ball restores order.

LIFE OBSERVATION

It might seem counterintuitive, but it's not always the biggest or strongest player who wins that second ball. Often, it's the player who reads the game the best and can anticipate where the ball is likely to go. Remember, the goal is to restore order from chaos as quickly as possible. Those who think ahead are best primed to do that.

At some point everyone's life is thrown into chaos. How can you regain some control? Can you remain calm in the heat of the moment and make the simple play that helps the team? Especially in youth soccer, all too often the second ball becomes the third ball, or the fourth ball, as some-one attempts to wildly kick it forward. It takes a smart player, however, to calm the game down by controlling it and playing it (often) backwards, to where her team has the most time and space to begin a new attack.

This involves teamwork, where we remember that we don't have to go it alone, and that the reality is there's always help. Sometimes in life there are challenges or confrontations, but the group can work together, each individual using her own strengths.

Again, it's typically not the tallest player who wins the second ball. Rather it's the one with vision, who can see where the ball is likely to go and recognize where the space is. She not only has the technical chops to bring the ball under control but also knows one of the cardinal rules of soccer; *she knows what to do with the ball before she gets it*, and consequently she can make the next play quickly. Remember, this area of the field is still congested. Immediately after winning the ball, she will be under pressure. Her job is to secure possession for her team and start an attack.

Restoring order also can mean taking a step back in order to see the bigger picture. In a soccer game this can be as simple as playing the ball backwards rather than trying to press forward into a tricky situation. In life we often need to take stock of things and regroup as we consider a new way forward.

When you're part of a team, everyone has certain roles. The player who goes up to win a header may have different physical qualities than the player who is able to gain control of the second ball. But still, everyone in the group is working together, and the way we do that is to bring our best qualities to the table.

In life, we aren't asked to be something we're not, we're simply tasked with being the best version of ourselves. If we concentrate on that, on focusing on what we can actually control, we'll find a way to help the team and restore order from chaos.

"In the midst of chaos, there is also an opportunity." – Sun Tzu

Chapter 29

DON'T BALL WATCH

———————— ⚽ ————————

Remembering priorities

"We consistently see that elite players spend vast amounts of time looking at areas of the field away from the ball. The best players in this game watch the game, whereas the not so good players watch the ball." – Gier Jordet, Norwegian sports psychologist

There are times when life seems to be overwhelming, and there's a natural tendency in those moments to either get distracted or to focus on the wrong thing when life gets chaotic. When we're stuck in these situations it can be hard to remember the most important thing that we're worried about, especially when our brain is struggling to juggle different priorities. Our eyes naturally gravitate toward what's right in front of us, but often the thing seemingly screaming for our attention is not necessarily where our focus should be.

A magician will distract his audience and have them focus on one thing so he can surprise them with "magic." By changing the focus of the spectators, he can conceal the trick. This happens in soccer all the time.

GAME SCENARIO

When defending in soccer, players sometimes end up seemingly mesmerized by the ball movement of the opposition. If the other team is strong in possession, it's almost as if the defenders become hypnotized by the ball, and when this happens, eventually defenders can lose their focus, concentrating on the ball rather than where the ball will be. This can lead to mental errors. Maybe they fail to mark a player; or they fail to take up good covering positions or block passing lanes. They get so wrapped up in one thing they fail to see the bigger picture happening around them.

Open space on a soccer field is prime real estate, and defenders really need to understand how to protect vulnerable areas of the field. Particularly during transitions, where reactions must be very quick, it's natural that defenders' focus turns to the ball. While this is important, the crucial thing is to consider where the ball is going (this is why coaches, given their experience, often don't look at where the ball is, but rather other parts of the field to see how their team is set up for the next phase of play).

Coaches know that in the heat of the moment, however, the players themselves naturally gravitate to the ball. If there is even a short lapse in concentration, the defenders may fail to account for the actual threat, such as a player running behind them on the far post, for example.

It goes without saying that in soccer the basic defensive objective is to prevent a goal from being scored, and obviously the ball is important (generally speaking, we want kids to keep their eyes on the ball as that's the thing we're trying to keep out of the net). But there are other factors that need to be accounted for, and if we fail to respond to them, we could be in trouble.

While defending as part of a team, your priority is contingent on the role you have in a particular situation, yet it is still aligned with defending principles. We discussed the idea of "First Man" before; that is, the nearest defender to the ball has the job of delaying the attack. The other defenders must decide what to do based on their own positioning. This is where "DON'T BALL WATCH" comes into play. If you're not close to the ball as a defender, you have other priorities. If you're an outside back on the side of the field opposite where the ball is, you need to tuck inside and watch for any attacking runs to the back post.

For that outside back, while that bright shiny ball may try to grab his attention, he has to realize that another teammate is dealing with it. Remember, the threat the outside back must contend with is not where the ball is now, but where it might go. During transitions the threat can evolve very quickly, so it's important for defenders to figure out their jobs fast. In this case, the priority is where the attacking run is coming from, and where it's going.

LIFE OBSERVATION

So many things happen in a soccer game at any given moment. Between player movement, chatter from teammates, opponents, and coaches, the on-field environment can be very chaotic. Not to belabor the point, but during transitions, this is even more so.

The ability to quickly recognize and respond appropriately to what needs to be done is such an important skill. This type of focus is something that everyone should learn, but in society today, it might be harder than it ever was, because in a world full of distractions, we are all bombarded by noise. It envelops our lives as we are constantly barraged by things that take us away from what we really need to focus on.

As a society, we've forgotten how to be silent. We've become addicted to the noise, allowing extraneous things to steal our focus. It takes discipline to ignore the noise and concentrate on what's important.

The ball that players tend to fixate on represents that bright shiny object that beguiles just about everyone at some point. If we're honest, I think we can agree that most of us can be transfixed by something that grabs our attention and distracts us from what's more important.

This begs the question; how do we know what's important? To reiterate the common theme in this book, in so many ways, sport is no different than life. Whether we know it or not, the lives we live are guided by principles. Established principles that we commit ourselves to make it easier to prioritize our activities to determine where we should put our focus. They clarify what's really important and help us reach our objectives. Even if we're not conscious of it, principles guide our decision-making and actions.

When kids develop a strong sense of character based on positive, life-affirming principles, it will be easier for them to say "no" to things that take them away from their objective and help them prioritize the things that lead them to their goal.

Just as defenders in the middle of a game must ask themselves what they must do in particular situations to prevent a goal, off the field we need to focus on what we are supposed to be doing. Always keeping in mind our objective helps us to prioritize and so not get distracted by that bright shiny object demanding our attention.

It's really easy to get caught up focused on the noise that surrounds us but keeping priorities in order helps keep us moving in the right direction. In this scenario on a soccer field, if the outside back stays alert and watches the far post, he'll have a better chance of cutting out a pass.

If we can teach kids the importance of understanding the bigger picture and so focus on the right thing, they can prioritize effectively, and they'll continue to concentrate their efforts towards their goal, despite whatever extraneous stuff tries to get in their heads.

This applies to the mundane as well as more serious activities. When you have the proper focus, you live a certain way. In the short term, that might simply mean that you do the next right thing, regardless of the situation.

Let's face it, it's easy to get distracted. Even something as simple as being on your phone during family dinner or playing one more video game instead of doing homework. Even driving – we might be so focused on GPS directions that we forget to use the turning signal – or fail to be aware of other cars, cyclists, pedestrians, etc. Even for students when simply taking a test, they can easily get bogged down trying to answer a single question and ultimately lose time on the overall exam.

At work, maybe it's the dings from your phone letting you know you have more emails that seemingly "demand" your "immediate" action, even though we know that there are more important things to do. All too often short-term "priorities" grab our attention and take our focus, and we lose sight of the bigger picture.

We end up getting distracted and disregard the warning signs of a pending problem, all because our gaze is directed elsewhere, often in irrelevant minutiae. Before we realize it, very serious matters that we should address are ignored because we engage in less important (or even unnecessary) things, and we lose our focus.

As a result, serious problems that are percolating beneath the surface boil over and we fail to notice before it's too late. This could manifest at work where we had an important long-term presentation for which we failed to effectively prepare, or a relationship issue with a loved one that was never resolved.

Young people come to understand as they get older that it may feel sometimes as if life is throwing a lot at them and it can be hard to determine what the next step should be. We adults know that it often feels like we are juggling one (or more!) balls too many. As children grow, they must learn that particularly in these moments, it's vital that they remember to recognize where their priorities really lie.

As life gets hectic, keeping your eyes on the bigger objective (regardless of what it is) will ensure that you can cut through the static that surrounds you and retain your focus on the important stuff (like preventing a goal).

"The things that matter most should never be at the mercy of the things that matter least." – Johann Wolfgang von Goethe

Chapter 30

MAKE THE SIMPLE PASS

———————— ⚽ ————————

Restoring order

"Soccer is a simple game. But the hardest thing to do is play soccer simply." – Johann Cruyff

The ball has been won after a tackle, and the ball-winner needs to do something positive with it. Her head is down, and she needs to make a decision quickly since she is under a lot of pressure from the team who just lost the ball. A simple concept (but one that can be hard to ingrain into players) is to pass the ball as soon as possible to the nearest teammate.

GAME SCENARIO

More often than not the player who won the ball had just moments before been busy defending aggressively, with her head down and her focus solely on winning the ball. For the last several moments, this has been her priority. Now that she has won it, she likely is not aware of what exactly is around her. She is probably trying to make sure she maintains control of the ball, but now what? All too often you see players who win the ball just blindly dribble forward only to give the ball away again. All the good work winning that ball is now lost. It's these sorts of 1v1 challenges that plague much of youth soccer.

The simple and effective solution, however, is to play a short pass to the nearest teammate. While you have had your head down fighting over the ball, your teammates have had their heads up and know what is around you, and they should be telling you where to pass the ball. They are in a much better position to determine where it should go next.

This is such a simple thing, but it's something that isn't done often enough. When you watch a game (even a professional game) you'll always see players win a ball, put their head down, and try to dribble like crazy. It doesn't matter if they're in a crowd of opposition, they just try to go it alone until they can see for themselves what the next play is. It's important to remember that the entire team has eyes, and their perspective is much wider! While you've had your head down winning the ball, they can provide the vision that you don't have.

There are so many times I watch a game (especially a youth game) where one player just refuses to make this simple pass and instead tries to dribble through a maze of players. Yes, there is that "one out of ten times" that it works, but in the vast majority of cases, it means that better chances are neglected.

We all know that person, the one who wants to be the hero (let's be honest – at times we *are* all that person). Sometimes we get so excited with a particular task we lose sight of the bigger picture. In winning the ball a player may get the feeling that she is (finally!) in control and so she tries to do something (anything!) she can. It takes a certain maturity to realize that no matter what our situation, we do have other options besides trying to dribble past three people with our heads down.

Winning the ball is incredibly important, but in the big scheme of things if the ball is lost again just after it was won, then what's the point? The moment of transition is useless unless possession is retained.

This is where simplicity really is essential. We mentioned this earlier; good players consistently ask themselves how they can help their team. What can they do at any given moment to put their team in a better position? In this case, the ball-winner must admit that she's tired. Chasing and finally winning the ball is taxing physically (think of how a player feels after she's just run a hard sprint), and consequently the player may need a moment to recharge.

If she tries to dribble her way out of danger, she exerts even more energy, growing more and more tired, which ultimately negatively impacts her decision-making. Losing the ball immediately after winning it is a psychological blow; it's frustrating and exhausting to put in so much effort only to give the ball away so quickly.

LIFE OBSERVATION

As we get older, we face so many challenges in life. All too often we tend to overthink the problem, rather than pick the easiest, simplest solution. We overcomplicate the issue, and in a sense panic, ultimately delaying a response rather than addressing the problem right away. We know we could take a small step forward but instead we fail to do the simplest, most straightforward thing immediately.

Remember, the moment of transition is important for both teams. For the team that has won the ball, there may be an opportunity to attack the opponent directly if the right decisions are made quickly. Conversely, the team that has lost possession must simultaneously try to win the ball back while getting organized defensively as soon as possible.

We should make it clear that by passing in this situation a player isn't passing responsibility; she's sharing it and making the best decision for the group. By including her teammates in this way, she demonstrates maturity and understanding that the simple, obvious solution is the easiest way out of trouble.

We spend so much time making life harder than it is (although admittedly, life can get pretty hard at times). All too often, though, it becomes a matter of perspective. When we can't see the bigger picture, sometimes we see too many obstacles in our way and think that in order to succeed we have to go straight through them. The reality is that sometimes the far simpler (and more effective) solution is to just go around them. The ball-winner who keeps her head down and tries to dribble through too many defenders is making the problem much more difficult than it really is. She can't see the problem from a different viewpoint because she's frozen in the middle of the storm. If she had a different perspective, there's a good chance that she could see the simple solution.

When you're in the middle of something it's easy to forget the bigger picture. You might "put your head down" and start trying to move forward, but then you make it harder to see other options. Without knowing it, you unconsciously limit yourself.

Moments of transition in soccer are moments of chaos. In this situation, can the player who won the ball remain calm and act quickly so that her team can start the next phase of the game? Surrounded by opponents desperate to regain the ball, can she relax, remain strong, and identify where the space is? Can she listen to her teammates, get her head up for a moment, and find where she can safely pass the ball to a teammate (and in so doing restore some order to the chaos)?

When you're in a situation where you're surrounded by mayhem, there is a natural instinctive desire to escape and get to safety as fast as you can. If you're in a burning building, you don't want to hang out and watch the furniture burn; you want to get to a safe place fast. The caveat of course is that it's important to remember that you can't panic, either. You need to stay as calm as possible while acting quickly. In soccer, a player attempting to dribble through a maze of players right after winning the ball is often panicking. When players do this, it's clear that they haven't thought things through. They keep their heads down and try to push forward – but the reality is they don't even know where they're going.

They weren't prepared; they just acted against their own interests. Instead of running out of a burning house to safety they just ran into another room where the smoke was coming from.

I mentioned awareness before; it's important here as well. Transition is all about restoring order; about figuring out the chaos and how to solve it. Today, much of the modern game revolves around celebrating the chaos of transitions rather than on the order of playing a possession-based style.

That's fine; styles of play come and go. The thing that doesn't change, though, is that coaches will always seek out players who can, in the heat of battle, remain calm and make the best play for their team. Intelligent players with a "soccer brain" are always in demand; players who recognize the situation they're in and understand what the simple solution is.

This calmness is needed throughout our lives. When the storms come, we instinctively look for individuals who can rise above the fear and calmly assess the situation and act quickly. All our lives we gain experience, preparation for the next moment. Learning not to panic, and the importance of staying even-keeled despite the challenges, enables us to make sense of the chaos and make prudent decisions fast.

"Calmness is the cradle of power." – Josiah Gilbert Holland, American novelist

Chapter 31

NEXT FIVE

———— ⚽ ————

Staying even-keeled

"The score is always zero - zero." – Michael Jordan

During a soccer game, it's a common belief that a team is vulnerable to giving up a goal shortly after a team has either scored or has given up a goal. In a low-scoring sport like soccer, goals leave a significant psychological effect, either one of joy or sorrow. For any player, it's critical to put that goal (regardless of which team scored) out of his mind, focus on the restart, and get back into the rhythm of the game.

GAME SCENARIO

Obviously, a goal can be scored at any point during a game, but let's say two teams have been playing for about 15 minutes and the game has been pretty even. Suddenly one team wins a free kick just outside the penalty area and scores a goal.

At this point you may hear the coach of the team that just scored yell, "Next Five!" as a reminder for his team to "get back to business." He wants to let the team know that, yes, it's great we scored, but there's a lot of time left and much to do. It's time to take a breath and simply begin again.

This admonition applies equally to the other side as well. The players need to remember that giving up a goal isn't the end of the world. The mental state of any athlete is so important, as the mind and body are interconnected. Coaches and athletes talk about the need for having a short memory. In the popular TV show "Ted Lasso," the coach explains to one of his players that he needs to "be a goldfish" because a goldfish only has a ten-second memory. It's so important for athletes to not dwell on the past.

Players who put their heads down after giving up a goal are signaling frustration to themselves and their teammates, and that frustration manifests into poor body language. If a player does not re-engage with the game quickly, his focus will be off, and he will be susceptible to making a mistake.

Again, even for the team that scored there is a risk of a mental breakdown. The jubilation of a goal can also lend itself to a false sense of security. It's easy to let the celebration linger in your mind after the restart, and this can take away a player's concentration.

Many coaches direct their teams with the adage that whether you're winning or losing, the score is always 0-0; you're always trying to score and defend to the best of your ability. The point is that players need to take events of the game in stride, so to speak. Regardless if the moment be one of triumph or sorrow, it's critical to find your focus and re-engage the senses as the game begins again.

LIFE OBSERVATION

We've spoken before about how responding to a mistake is more important than the mistake itself. This applies here as well, but this is more about the need to remain steady and focused on the task at hand. I think most people have heard the expression about "keeping an even keel." The keel, which runs along the bottom of a boat, is designed to ensure steady and balanced sailing. Good sailors seek to maintain an even keel, which provides stability and control.

Soccer players need to be even-keeled, particularly after pivotal moments in a game. Likewise, all of us need to do this in our daily lives. How many people do you know who get visibly angry and fly off the handle over seemingly minor things? This response seldom helps anyone find a solution to a problem. Virile, overly emotional responses tend to be counterproductive; they serve to push others away and disconnect the person from the group.

Crazy highs or despondent lows take us away from the task at hand. Responding to one event unnaturally makes us less reliable and detaches us from the world around us. Yes, we're still physically in the environment, but mentally and emotionally we're somewhere else. Allowing our emotions to take over means we act less like adults and more like children, and the focus becomes self-centered and inward. Rather than controlling our emotions and returning to what we were doing, we lose sight of what's important at that moment.

All too often we fail to recognize that we have a role to play, regardless of failures or successes. Life throws a lot at us, both good and bad. Sometimes we experience exceptionally high moments as well as terribly low moments. But still, life goes on. Of course we react to these events, but always with the realization that tomorrow is another day.

"Games are won by players who focus on the playing field - not by those whose eyes are glued to the scoreboard." – Warren Buffet

WATER BREAK: SPREAD OUT

————— ⚽ —————

O f all that you hear on a soccer field, this is likely the one most often heard, especially at the youngest ages. We've all seen it – the clump of players and dust surrounding what must be the ball (it becomes hard to see with all those players in the way!). The image is something like Pigpen from Charlie Brown, slowly moving across the field. Inevitably the coach (and not a few of the parents) yell, "Spread out!"

It is obvious to adults that the players should spread out so they can pass to each other, but the fact is that the youngest kids have difficulty passing (or simply, and understandably, don't want to). What are we saying when we tell kids this? It's important to remember here that we're typically talking about the youngest ages, up to U8, maybe. At these ages proper passing technique with the inside of the foot is biomechanically challenging (it's hard for young kids to turn their foot to the side and complete a proper push pass). And remember, kids at these ages are self-centered (this is normal). They want to dribble the ball, and we should allow them to do so. The confidence and skill set they develop from controlling the ball and dribbling through "the swarm" will serve them well as they develop further.

This call heard from the touchlines is obviously well-intentioned, but it's really important to let the kids figure this out. I think a lot of the time we watch that swarm and we think, wait, that's not what the game is supposed to look like. Well, that's true, but at the youngest ages it probably shouldn't look like professional soccer either. After all, the artwork hanging on the family refrigerator doesn't look like a Rembrandt, and we don't get too upset about that!

What "spread out" actually means is that the adults want the kids to pass the ball. The reality is that this shouldn't be a coaching priority at the youngest ages. During these early phases of development, the kids should be mastering other skills, like ball control and manipulation. If they can master that, ultimately learning to pass the ball will be easy.

Eventually kids will learn concepts of the game such as the importance of spacing. At the youngest ages, though, let them experience the simple joy of running around outside.

Sometimes parents find themselves trying to "hurry up" certain stages of development in kids. What can make this more problematic is the simple fact that every kid develops at different speeds. Maturity is not a catch-all term, either. A child's physical maturity may develop faster than his emotional or social maturity. Both parents and coaches must take this into consideration. A child who is more advanced in mental maturity may be more "coachable," even though his physical growth may appear slower.

I remember when my first child was born, older parents kindly told me to enjoy everything because time goes by so fast. I think all new parents are told something similar, and it's so true. The trouble is that we sometimes forget this and so try to hurry things up as we desperately want kids to "get it (whatever "it" is)." While we certainly want to help them grow and develop, we must remember that this is their experience, and while it's ok to be with them and guide them – ultimately, it's their game and we have to let them enjoy it at their pace.

The lesson here is really just a reminder for all of us adults to remember that at the end of the day, soccer is just a game, and it's ok to let kids run around and enjoy themselves.

CONCLUSION: POST-GAME TALK

⚽

After a game of youth soccer ends, it is typically followed by both a post-game talk between the coach and the players, and the car ride home. The post-game talk should be brief, so this conclusion will be as well.

Immediately after a game, the players are tired. They won't be able to absorb much information, so the talk needs to be short and sweet, and needs to cover just a few points. First, praise effort. Effort is what truly fuels the drive for self-improvement and inspires teammates. Effort makes a talented player an even better player – it is a quality needed outside the playing field. When a child's talent is not enough to achieve success, those who are lauded for their effort will continue to seek a positive outcome (rather than give up).

Second, provide *constructive* feedback and solicit input from players (they were the ones in the game, after all). The key here is to ensure that the players' own self-esteem is not negatively affected. In life, there are no final victories, and no final defeats. Everything in life represents a learning opportunity, if we have the willingness to seek self-improvement.

Lastly, simply bring attention to the next game. This game is over, now focus on the next one. One of the great things about sport is that there is always another game. Whatever the result, it's now in the past and it's time to look toward the future.

For parents during the ride home, they must remember that the kids will be processing their own emotions, so it's important to simply remember that now is the time to just be "Mom" and "Dad." Even parent coaches should recognize that the game is over so it's time to take off the coach's hat.

For the players, once the game is over, their physical, mental, and emotional investment in the activity needs time to recharge. The peaks and valleys of the competition they've experienced can begin to even out, and their focus on other interests and people naturally take precedence. After the final whistle, kids forget the result *within minutes*. They know what happened during the game (and certainly do not need to experience the blow-by-blow retelling once inside the minivan pressure-cooker).

Remember, whatever level your child is playing, I'm pretty sure the game you just watched isn't going to decide the World Cup. As parents, we recognize that one game – regardless of how "big" it may be – is just one moment of a child's life. The focus of both coaches and parents must have a longer frame of view.

As a parent, when the game is over, take a cue from your child and recognize what he already knows. He has invested all of himself into that activity for the length of the game. Now it's done and it's time to move on to something else. As tempting as it may be, don't rehash the past; simply encourage another positive influence or interest in your child's life. For me, the best thing a parent can say to their kid after a game is simply, "I love watching you play."

Remember, **the number one reason children play youth sports is because it's fun**. Kids do not need or want parents to "coach" them following a game. They simply want support. When you were a child and you met your friends at the park to play pick-up games, did your parents greet you at the door with questions about how you played or if you won? Of course not. They simply asked, "Did you have fun?" That question is just as appropriate immediately after an organized game.

Parents should remember that at the end of the day they are actually *guests* at their kids' games. The young players have already received instruction from their coaches, and all too often parental "guidance" directly contradicts what their coaches want them to do.

"Praise for effort and progress motivates students, praise for ability ends up undermining their motivation. This is because praise for ability tells them that they always have to look smart, so they stay away from hard work and get discouraged when they make mistakes." – Carol Dweck, American psychologist

INJURY TIME

---------- ⚽ ----------

"They think it's all over...it is now! – Kenneth Wolstenhome, English football commentator

Y ou thought it was over! Well, soccer is different from other sports in that the time is not kept on a scoreboard, but is controlled by the referee, who accounts for interruptions like player substitutions and injuries. Consequently, you never *really* know when the game will end.

I love the game of soccer; I played it, watched it, and read about it. I practically breathed the game - so much so that my wife included my love for soccer in her wedding vows - and most people know me as a soccer fanatic.

The love I had for the sport as a kid was very basic and natural. I just loved playing; I didn't really begin to understand the nuance and the beauty of the sport until I was older. In my young adulthood I devoured soccer statistics and news and watched an untold number of matches. At that point I wasn't really making the connections between soccer tactics and how the lessons learned on the field are so applicable to life.

As a father, I was able to coach all four of my kids at some point during their childhood and I was an observer to many hundreds of hours of my kids playing for other coaches on a number of teams at various levels of play. It is those hours, as well as the time I have spent reflecting on my own life in the last few years, that prompted me to write this book.

If you have read this book all the way to the end (and I am glad that you did!), you may be under the illusion that I now have life all figured out. Let me put those thoughts to rest. The fact is, much of what I now understand has come from writing this book and reflecting on a lifetime of my own mistakes...and I am referring to the ones that I've made OFF the soccer field. Looking back, I wish that I had known when in life to Dribble, or when to Turn. Had I been better at Getting Behind the Ball or Making The Simple Passes in Life, I know that there are situations for me that could have yielded better results.

These are lessons I've learned. I have written them down in part because we are all essentially a work in progress. I do hope you took some practical soccer knowledge from this book, whether you are a coach, a player, or a fan. More importantly though, I hope you found some "words of wisdom" from the text that you can apply to your own life. Personal experience is life's greatest teacher, but we can also learn from others (so long as we're willing).

"I learned all about life with a ball at my feet." – Ronaldinho, Brazilian World Cup winner

Acknowledgements

I am sincerely thankful to the many people who supported me in writing this book. Those closest to me know that it has been long in the making. My love for soccer has always been evident, and I have spent years learning and developing the ideas that I wanted to share in a book. The influence on me by the people mentioned here is immeasurable both in the ways it formed my ideas and in how I was helped to make them make sense to a larger audience.

I am grateful to my parents, George and Edda Roth, who supported me in all my endeavors and patiently watched me embrace this beautiful game when I was a kid. I am thankful for all the volunteer coaches who stepped up in the 70s and 80s (including my dad) to try to teach kids how to play a sport they themselves had never actually played.

I am thankful for my family, especially Tami, my wife of 27 years without whom it's safe to say this book would never have been finished. She supported me through many years of writing about this thing that I love and ultimately was instrumental in helping to finalize the book. She somehow effectively became her own publishing house, performing editing, illustrating, formatting, and design duties like a pro. More importantly, she saw the times I missed the mark and patiently encouraged me to make connections I failed to see. In addition, the lessons I learned from my own children – Brendan, Devin, Morgan, and Connor – served to illuminate some of life's mysteries and their connections to the game. No father could be prouder; they never cease to amaze me.

I am grateful for my friends at the Saint Joan of Arc Writers Group, especially Father Al Scescki for hosting the group, and Tess Cesari, Karen Kier, Neil Ott, Lisa Perrotti, and Patrick Taylor who listened, offered opinions and inspired me with their own works. I want to thank a host of people who volunteered to read and offer suggestions during the writing process, such as Rebecca Burk, Joe Eisenhauer, Matt Loper, Christoper Parillo, Ceil Perretta, Phil Sanchez, and Brian Thomas, and also Kate Hannisian, whose professional editing and insight were invaluable.

I want to acknowledge the multitude of youth soccer coaches I've known throughout the years working at every level in the soccer landscape, from recreational to club to middle and high school coaches. These folks wield tremendous influence on kids and their positive impact on my own children was significant. I learned a great deal from my own interactions with them. There have been too many to mention but I would be remiss if I didn't specifically recognize Bill Becher, John Carbaugh, Dennis Clark, Roy Gesford, Dave Hickey, Damon Kaylor, Gerry Lynch, Pete Murray, Jason Pelletier, Drew Rohacek, Tyler Schleig, and Keith Walt.

Finally, I am simply grateful for the beautiful game. Who knew that chasing a ball around a big grass field could hold such mystery?

www.ingramcontent.com/pod-product-compliance
Lightning Source LLC
Chambersburg PA
CBHW070326130626

46556CB00007B/2745